SCOTS
IN THE
CARIBBEAN

1600 - 1900

BY
DAVID DOBSON

CLEARFIELD

Copyright © 2025
by David Dobson
All Rights Reserved

Published for Clearfield Company by
Genealogical Publishing Company
Baltimore, Maryland
2025

ISBN: 9780806359786

INTRODUCTION

Scotland has had social and economic links with the Caribbean for round 400 years. Initially, economic links or trade between Scotland and the English colonies were very limited because of the monopoly on trade held by English merchants based on the English Navigation Acts. These laws were aimed specifically at the Dutch, England's principal rival in the seventeenth century. However, the political union of Scotland and England in 1707 removed all such restrictions and enabled Scots to emigrate to or trade with the colonies without restriction.

Emigration to the Caribbean by Scots was minimal until the middle of the eighteenth century. Most of the Scots in the West Indies had been transported there as prisoners of war, political undesirables or common criminals, such as Jacobites, Cromwellian captives, Covenanters, as well as men and women taken from various jails in Scotland. Some Scottish colonials were entrepreneurs, like the ones who developed sugar and other plantations, and some were from landed families with funds to invest. Men recruited in Scotland, often through newspapers such as the *Aberdeen Journal*, were expected to have commercial skills or agricultural experience, often to run plantations for absentee owners.

The situation changed in 1763 with the end of the Seven Years War between France and Britain when certain islands, such as St. Lucia and Tobago, previously French, became British and the British government promoted settlement there. Small numbers of Scots went to the Dutch and Danish West Indies, in places such as St. Eustatia or St. Croix. Britain also acquired Dutch colonies on the east coast of South America, namely, Demerara, Essequibo, and Berbice, where vast sugar plantations were developed. In that respect, Scottish emigration to the Caribbean differed from colonization to North America, which was generally undertaken by families. Scottish emigrants to the Caribbean were mostly men who chose to leave their families at home, possibly due to the unhealthy climate in the West Indies. Ships voyaging between Scotland and the Caribbean illustrate trade routes from Scotland, with passengers and manufactures such as linen and metalware on the outbound voyages, and raw materials, generally cotton, tobacco, sugar, and mahogany, on the return.

This book provides an overview of Scots and the Caribbean; however, looking for more specialised source material dealing with particular islands, the following books of mine, all published by Clearfield Company, are available – *The People of Jamaica, 1655-1855*; *The People of Barbados, 1625-1875*; *The People of the Leeward Islands, 1620-1860*; *The People of the Windward islands, Trinidad, Tobago, and Curacao, 1620-1860*; *Barbados and Scottish Links, 1627-1877*; *Scots in the West Indies, 1707-1857, Part One* and *Part Two;* and *The Original Scots Colonists of Early America, Caribbean Supplement, 1611-1707*.

David Dobson, Dundee, Scotland, 2025

Scottish newspapers carried advertisements encouraging emigration to the British colonies, for example the following extracts from the 'Aberdeen Journal' –'Wanted immediately for the island of Grenada, a house carpenter and wright. Any such, well recommended, will find suitable encouragement by applying to Alexander Ross junior, a merchant in Aberdeen.' [Aberdeen Journal, #1872, November 1783.] and 'Wanted for Dominica in the West Indies, a house carpenter, well qualified in that business and understanding something of machinery. Such a one property recommended will hear of good encouragement by applying to William Forbes in Aberdeen.' [Aberdeen Journal, #1595, August 1778.]

REFERENCES

ABR Ayr Burgh Records
ACA Aberdeen Burgh Archives
AJ Aberdeen Journal, series
AUL Aberdeen University Library
BM Book of Mackay, [Edinburgh, 1896]
BM Blackwood's Magazine, series
CM Caledonian Mercury, series
DAC Dumfries Archive Centre
DC Daily Courant, Edinburgh, series
DUA Dundee University Archives
EEC Edinburgh Evening Courant, series
EMG Edinburgh Medical Graduates
EMR Edinburgh Marriage Register
EUL Edinburgh University Library
F. Fasti Ecclesiae Scoticanie, [Edinburgh, 1915]
FF Family of Forbes, [Aberdeen 1946]
FH Fife Herald, series
FJ Fife Journal, series
FSS Family of Skene of Skene, [Aberdeen, 1887]
FU Family of Urquhart, [Aberdeen, 1946]
GCA Glasgow City Archives
GM Gentleman's Magazine, series
HCA Highland Council Archives, Inverness
HCAS High Court of the Admiralty of Scotland
HS History Scotland, series
IRO Island Record Office, Jamaica

KCA King's College Archives, Aberdeen
MAGU Matriculation Albums of Glasgow University
MCA Marischal College Archives, Aberdeen
NLJ National Library of Jamaica
NLS National Library of Scotland
NRAS National Register of Archives, Scotland
NRS National Records of Scotland
OA Orkney Archives
PSAS Proceedings of the Society of Antiquaries of Scotland
PJ People's Journal, series
RAK Danish Archives, Copenhagen
RSSP Recovering Scotland's Slavery Past, [Edinburgh,2015]
S The Scotsman, series
SAU St Andrews University
SL South Leith Irregular Marriages [Edinburgh 1968]
SRA Strathclyde Regional Archives
SS Surnames of Scotland, [New York, 1946]
TNA The National Archives, London
TOF Thanage of Fermartyn. [Aberdeen, 1894]
RGG Register of Glasgow Graduates
UA University of Aberdeen

These two maps are taken from Volume XXIV, September 1763, of *The Gentleman's Magazine*. *The Gentleman's Magazine* was founded in 1739 and remained in its original format until around 1825, when a new format was used. It is still in print today. The engraver for these maps is believed to have been Andrew Bell, who had a shop in Mary King's Close off of the Royal Mile in Edinburgh. Mary King's Close has long had a reputation for hauntings and urban legends and is now a tourist attraction.

ABERCROMBY, GEORGE, a physician in Mexico around 1770.
[NRS.NRAS.OOO2]

ABERCROMBY, GEORGE, in Rotterdam and in Mexico, letters dated 1762 to 1764, [NRS.GD185.6.2]; a physician in Mexico around 1770. [NRS.NRAS.OOO2]; in Mexico a letter to Sir Robert Abercromby in 1774. [NRS.GD185.3]

ABERCROMBY, LUISA, in Mexico, a letter to Sir Robert Abercromby, her uncle, 25 July 1777. [NRS.GD185.8]

ABERNETHY, ALEXANDER, a merchant in Broadgait, Aberdeen, trading with Jamaica in 1780. [AJ]

ABERNETHY, GEORGE, a merchant in Aberdeen and in Jamaica, a deed in 1751. [NRS.RD4.177.311]

ADAM, HENRY, an engineer in Mexico, heir to his grandmother Mary Robertson, wife of John Galt a mason in Govan, Glasgow, who died on 23 November 1859, 8 November 1900. [NRS.S/H]

ADAMS, JOHN, a merchant in Glasgow trading with Jamaica in 1756. [NRS.AC7.48.930]

ADAMSON, GEORGE an accountant, born 1825, second son of .....Mr Adamson of the Inland Revenue in Forres, Moray, died on Golden Grove Estate in Jamaican 20 September 1850. [IA]

ADARE, ROBERT, from Galloway, probate 29 December 1692 in Barbados. [RB.6.3.63]

ADDISON, JOHN, a merchant in Montrose, Angus, trading with Antigua, in 1754. [NRS.AC7.46.51]

AIKMAN, ANDREW, in Kingston, Jamaica, a letter to his brother John Aikman, re the French refugees from Hispaniola, dated 10 August 1793. [NRS.GD1.1429.1/1]

AIKMAN, W. G., father of a son who was born in Belize, British Honduras on 11 June 1882

AIRD, JOHN MACKENZIE, in Grenada, son and heir of Alexander Aird a merchant in Invergordon, in Easter Ross, 13 March 1850, also nephew and heir of George Mackenzie in Culcragie, 19 February 1856. [NRS.S/H]; also heir to his cousin Margaret MacKenzie in Invergordon, 19 February 1856, and heir to his grand-uncle George MacKenzie in Invergordon, 20 February 1860. [NRS.S/H]

AITCHISON, JOHN, a merchant in Grenada, died in Connecticut in 1770. [SM.32.630]

AITKEN, CHARLES, a merchant in St Croix, Danish West Indies, in 1771. [ANY.1.128]

AITKEN, JAMES J., son of Andrew Aitken a farmer in Carnock in Fife, died on Plantation Albion in Berbice on 27 September 1848. [FH]

AITKEN, JOHN GEORGE, son of John Aitken a physician in Edinburgh, died in Demerara on 3 August 1803. [DPCA.73] [AJ.2919]

AITKEN, JOHN, youngest son of … Aitken in Carneil, Fife, died in Havanna, Cuba, on 11 March 1856. [FH]

AITKEN, ROBERT, a surgeon, son of Robert Aitken a lawyer in Cupar, Fife, died in Jamaica on 12 August 1841. [FH]

AIKMAN, W. G., father of a son who was born in Belize, British Honduras on 11 June 1882

ALEXANDER, ARTHUR HARVEY, graduated MA from Aberdeen University in 1862, son of Charles Alexander a planter in Grenada. [MCA]

ALEXANDER, or LLOYD, CHRISTINA, in St Lucia, heir of Marie Jean Alexander in St Lucia, 22 February 1839. [NRS.S/H]; as widow of Ebenezer Lloyd a merchant in London, later in St Lucia, sister and heir of Robertina Alexander who died in St Lucia on 14 January 1866, 14 February 1867. [NRS.S/H]

ALEXANDER, HARRY, purchased land in Antigua in 1765. [NRS.GD1.32.38.27]

ALEXANDER, JANET, was heir of Marie Jean Alexander in St Lucia, 22 February 1839. [NRS.S/H]

ALEXANDER, or LYON, JEAN, in Greenock, daughter and heir of William Alexander a cooper from Greenock, later in Tobago, 21 April 1837. [NRS.SH]

ALEXANDER, JEANETTE MARY, in St Lucia, sister and heir of Robertina Alexander in St Lucia who died on 14 January 1866, 14 February 1867. [NRS.S/H]

ALEXANDER, ROBERT, in Jamaica, son and heir of his mother Janet Black, wife of Thomas Alexander a merchant in Maybole, Ayrshire, 17 April 1804. [NRS.S/H]; also, grandson and heir to Quintin Black in Brockloch and Lochstoun, Ayrshire, 17 April 1804. [NRS.S/H]

ALEXANDER, ROBERTINA, heir to Marie Jean Alexander in St Lucia, 22 February 1839. [NRS.S/H]

ALEXANDER, WILLIAM, a merchant trading between Greenock and Jamaica in 1746, and between Port Glasgow and Jamaica in 1748. [NRS.E504.15.2, and E504.28.4]

ALLAN, COLIN, MD, died in Demerara in 1805. [SM.68.565] [AJ.2991]

ALLAN, GEORGE, in St Croix, Danish West Indies, cousin and heir of George Allan, son of Reverend Alexander Allan in Edinburgh, 28 February 1820. [NRS.S/H]

ALLAN, JAMES, master of the Thomas of Glasgow and son of James Allan a watchmaker in Aberdeen, died in Demerara on 10 September 1841.[AJ]

ALLAN, JOHN, born 1728, son of Hugh Allan a merchant in Kilmarnock, Ayrshire, died in Surinam in 1813. [EA.5194.13]

ALLEN, ROBERT, a merchant in Barbados, sister and heir of Christine Allen or Stewart, widow of Reverend Peter Stewart in Auchtergaven, 15 February 1755. [NRS.S/H]

ALLAN, WILLIAM, a merchant in Paisley, cousin and heir of George Allan in Grenada, 26 December 1834. [NRS.S/H]

ALLAN, WILLIAM, born 1877 only son of William Allan in Peterculter, Aberdeenshire, an overseer on Plantation Uitogt in Demerara, died on 22 August 1899. [AJ]

ALLEYNE, JAMES HOLDER, from Barbados, graduated MD from Edinburgh University in 1822. [EMG]

ALSTEIN, FREDERICK A. M., born 1815, died in Demerara on 9 March 1860. [Dean gravestone, Edinburgh]

ALSTEIN, FREDERICK ROBERT, born 1842, son of Frederick A. M. Falstein and his wife Janet, died in Demerara on 13 March 1866, [Dean gravestone, Edinburgh]

ALVES, THOMAS, in Jamaica, heir to his Inverness great grandfather Thomas Alves of Shipland, a merchant, 8 February 1792. [NRS.S/H]

ANDERSON, ALEXANDER, from Aberdeenshire, an estate manager on Carriacou near Grenada in 1782. [PSAS.114.494]

ANDERSON, ANDREW, from Aberdeenshire, an estate manager on Carriacou near Grenada in 1782. [PSAS.114.494]

ANDERSON, ANDREW, a naval architect in Antigua, heir and uncle of Alexandrina Anderson, daughter of Alexander Anderson of Newton, 28 July 1769, [NRS.S/H]

ANDERSON, DAVID, only son of David Anderson a merchant in Dundee, died in Curacao, Dutch West Indies, on arrival from Monte Video on 30 November 1807. [SM.70.317]

ANDERSON, ELIZABETH, widow of H. Watson of Torsance a Writer to the Signet, was heir to her uncle John Watson, a merchant in Jamaica who died on 20 August 1850, 11 November 1851. [NRS.S/H]

ANDERSON, HENRY JOHN, in Falmouth, Jamaica, nephew and heir of John Anderson in Belleville who died on 10 May 1847, 21 May 1866. [NRS.S/H]

ANDERSON, JANET STORY, wife of Reverend Francis Forbes in British Guiana, died on the Plantation de Willem on 9 March 1847. [EEC.21493]

ANDERSON, JOHN, master of the Providence of Glasgow, arrived in Glasgow from Antigua in 1672. [NRS.E72.10.2]

ANDERSON JOHN, from Boharm in Banffshire, a surgeon in St Michael's parish, Barbados, probate 2 December 1714, Barbados [RB6.41.9]

ANDERSON, JOHN, born 1781, son of John Anderson, a farmer in Easter Buchanty, and his wife Ann Moir [1750-1801] died in Honduras in March 1813. [Monzie gravestone, Perthshire]

ANDERSON, Reverend JOHN, born in Nairnshire, minister of a Presbyterian Church in New Amsterdam in British Guiana, by 1835, died there on 6 July 1840. [F.7.673][AJ]

ANDERSON, MARGARET, daughter and heir of David Anderson a wright in Antigua, 20 November 1777. [NRS.S.H]

ANDERSON, POLLY, daughter and heir of David Anderson a wright in Antigua, 20 November 1777. [NRS.S.H]

ANDERSON, THOMAS, MD in Trinidad, son and heir of James Anderson a surgeon in Antigua, 20 October 1829. [NRS.S/H]

ANDERSON, WILLIAM, a student at Marischal College in Aberdeen around 1802, son of Henry Anderson in Grenada. [MCA]

ANDERSON, WILLIAM, in Dominica, son and heir of William Anderson a merchant in London, 28 January 1822, [NRS.S/H], also, heir to his aunt Rachel Anderson, daughter of Henry Anderson a farmer in Broughton, Edinburgh, 22 March 1824, [NRS.S/H]; also, heir to his aunt Jean Anderson, wife of William Sommers an innkeeper in Edinburgh, 22 March 1824; also heir to his aunt Margaret Anderson, wife of John Bogue a Writer to the Signet, 22 March 1824, [NRS.S/H]; and heir to his uncle Henry Anderson, son of Henry Anderson a farmer in Broughton, 22 March 1824. [NRS.S/H]

ANDREW, Mrs ELIZABETH, daughter of Andrew Millar a Writer to the Signet, wife of Richard J. Andrew a merchant in Belize, Honduras, died there on 19 March 1831. [EEC.18646]; her husband died there on 13 February 1832. [EEC.18782]

ANGLIN, PHILIP, from Jamaica, graduated MD from Edinburgh University in 1823. [EMG]

ANGUS, ANDREW, in St Kitts, heir to Alexander Mein a surgeon in Dalkeith, Midlothian, 18 December 1754. [NRS.S/H]

ANGUS, WILLIAM, born 10 February 1771, son of William Angus and his wife Elspeth Mortimer in Aberdeen, was educated at King's College, Aberdeen, from 1784 until 1788, a surgeon in Jamaica. [KCA]

ARBUCKLE, WILLIAM, in Falkirk, Stirlingshire, nephew and heir to John Steven a millwright in Trinidad, 21 March 1845. [NRS.S/H]

ARBUTHNOTT, JOHN, born in 1762, son of Robert Arbuthnott and his wife Mary Urquhart in Aberdeenshire, a merchant in Rotterdam who died in Curacao, Dutch West Indies, in 1785. [FU.207]

ARBUTHNOTT, WILLIAM, born 1766, son of Robert Arbuthnott of Haddo-Rattray in Aberdeenshire, and his wife Mary Urquhart, a planter on Carriacao in the Grenadines, from 1783, returned to Scotland before 1804. [PSAS.14.482]

ARCHER, JAMES, second son of George Archer, a physician in Jamaica, matriculated at Glasgow University in 1812. [RGG]

ARCHER, JAMES, a stocking weaver in Nottingham, England, brother and heir of Andrew Archer in Jamaica, 6 November 1826. [NRS.S/H]

ARMOUR, ROBERT, a surgeon in Trinidad, brother and heir of Hugh Armour a skipper in Irvine, Ayrshire, 1 May 1823. [NRS.S/H]

ARMSTRONG, A., from St Cruz, (St Croix, Danish West Indies), graduated MD from Edinburgh University in 1815. [EMG]

ARMSTRONG, EDWARD, in St Lucy's, Barbados, in 1679. [TNA.CO1.44/47]

ARMSTRONG, JOHN, father of Rachel Armstrong who was baptised in St Lucy's, Barbados, on 5 August 1678.]TNA.CO1.44/47]

ARMSTRONG, JOHN, a writer [lawyer] from Edinburgh, in Jamaica in 1778. [NRS.HCAS.AC7.56]

ARMSTRONG, THOMAS GENT, born 1780, died 21 July 1812. [St Peter's, Speight Town, Barbados, gravestone]

ARNOLD, WILLIAM, from Port Antonio, Jamaica, graduated MD at King's College, Aberdeen, on 29 October 1821, a fellow of the Royal College of Physicians of Edinburgh in 1822, later an author. [KCA]

ARTHUR, CHARLES, master of the Charles of Glasgow from Port Glasgow bound for the West Indies in April 1691. [NRS.E72.15.22]

ARTHUR, GEORGE, of the Union Bank in Auchtermuchty in Fife, emigrated to Barbados in June 1850. [FJ]

ARTHUR, JAMES INNES, born 22 July 1785 in Resolis, son of Reverend Robert Arthur and his wife Anne Munro, settled in Demerara, died there on 20 August 1816. [F.7.19]

ARTHUR, LAUCHLAN, from Bo'ness in West Lothian, assistant to the Hand in Hand Insurance Company, died in Georgetown, Demerara, on 29 August 1881. [S.11919]

ARTHUR, ROBERT, master of the Fortune of Glasgow from Antigua to Port Glasgow in 1715. [NRS.HCAS.AC9.584; AC7.22.440]

ARTHUR, ROBERT, born in Resolis, son of Reverend Robert Arthur and his wife Anne Munro, settled in Berbice, in Cromarty, Easter Ross, on 3 July 1829. [S.994] on 20 August 1816. [F.7.19]

AULD, ALEXANDER, of Carcoside, Dumfries-shire, formerly a planter in Demerara, testament 1821. [NRS.PS3.14.383]

AULD, MATILDA, daughter of Alexander Auld of Carcaside, lately a planter in Demerara, 5 January 1826. [NRS.PS3.14.383]

AULD, ROBERT OGILVIE, born 1806, died in Guanesavi, Durango, Mexico, on 30 October 1846. [EEC.21451]

AUSTIN, JANE GORDON, in Demerara, a Discharge to Theodore Gordon dated 5 March 1880. [NRS.RD

BAILLIE, JAMES, from Grenada, married Miss Colleen Campbell, in Edinburgh on 20 April 1772. [EMR]

BAIRD, ROBERT, in Surinam, letters to Andrew Russell a Scottish merchant in Rotterdam, Zealand, 1689. [NRS.RH1.2.772]

BAIRD, MASON, and Company, manufacturers in Aberdeen, trading with Dominica between 1810 and 1829. [NRS.CS96.3877]

BALFOUR, JOHN, in Tobago, a bond in favour of Sir G. Aitkinson, dated 6 September 1829. [NRS.RD.444.431]

BALDWYN Captain, master of the Dolphin from Jamaica bound for New York was captured by the Spanish near Cape Nicholas, Hispaniola, on 18 October 1718. [NRS.GD158.1679]

BALLANTYNE, JAMES, eldest son of James Ballantyne a merchant in Campbeltown, Argyll, died in Demerara on 21 April 1802. [SM.64.708]

BALLOCH, WILLIAM, the Secretary of Jamaica, his widow Elizabeth Dunkley, born 1782, died on 6 August 1857, [Restalrig gravestone, Edinburgh]

BARBOUR, MARGARET, in Houston, Renfrewshire, sister and heir of Robert Lyle in Lottery in Jamaica, 26 August 1839. [NRS.S/H]

BARCLAY, BEATRIX BESSY, wife of Andrew Houton in Kelty in Fife, sister and heir of James Barclay a merchant in Jamaica, 14 July 1750. [NRS.S/H]

BARCLAY, CHARLES GEORGE, a merchant in Jamaica, son and heir of Charles Barclay a farmer in Inchbroom, Elgin, Moray, who died on 27 October 1854, 9 July 1855. [NRS.S/H]

BARCLAY, CLEMENTINA, wife of R. Cockerton in Trinidad, daughter and heir of Thomas Barclay an auctioneer in Glasgow who died on 22 May 1853, 28 October 1854. [NRS.S/H]

BARCLAY, JAMES, in Jamaica, brother and heir of George Barclay of Cairnes in Aberdeenshire who died in June 1756, 23 August 1757. [NRS.S/H]

BARCLAY, JAMES, born 1790 in Montrose, Angus, died in Bermuda on 11 March 1831. [St Peter and St George gravestone, Bermuda]

BARCLAY, JANET, wife of George Henderson a gardener in Kirkland, sister and heir of James Barclay a merchant in Jamaica, 15 November 1750. [NRS.S/H]

BARCLAY, WILLIAM, son of Charles Barclay a farmer in St Andrews in Moray, was educated at Marischal College in Aberdeen, later a merchant in the West Indies. [MCA]

BARDNER, ELIZABETH, daughter of John Bardner a warehouseman in Dunfermline, Fife, married Sergeant Thomas Hart, in Craigton, Jamaica, on 18 January 1869. [DP]

BARNET, JOHN, a builder in London, nephew and heir of John Mackay a mason in Jamaica, 4 October 1854. [NRS.S/H]

BARR, ROBERT, in Jamaica, son of Peter Barr in Hutchesontown, Glasgow, a letter, 1846. [GCA.GB23D1710]

BARTLETT, PATRICK, from Banff, settled in Carriocou near Grenada, later in London, an executor of Joseph Cumming in 1799. [NRS.CC8.8.131]

BAXTER, ISABELLA, only daughter of Richard Baxter in Demerara and grand-daughter of Andrew MacFarlane in Jamaica, married Alexander Heastie a surgeon of the Royal Navy, on 20 January 1818. [DPCA.809]

BAYNE, RICHARD, died in Barbados on 3 September 1767. [St Philip's gravestone]

BEACH, D., on St Croix, Danish West Indies, father of Rachael Beach, born 1814, died on 3 November 1829. [Restalrig gravestone, Edinburgh]

BECKETT, PETER, purchased land in Antigua in 1765.
[NRS.GD1.32.38.27]

BEGLIE, ALEXANDER, a surgeon in Surinam, a sasine in Edinburgh, dated 9 August 1832. [NRS.RS38.174]

BEGRIE, EDWARD WILLIAM, in Nassau, New Providence, in the Bahamas, heir of David Begrie, also to William Begrie, and to Alexander Begtrie, all in Edinburgh, 11 November 1881. [NRS.S/H]

BELL, GEORGE, was bound for the West Indies from Rotterdam, testament dated 24 January 1628. [GAR.NA.128.183.496]

BELL, Captain PHILIP, was bound for St Lucia to be minister there in January 1640. [NRS.GD504.9.97]

BELL, WILLIAM, in Port Glasgow, master of the Jessie trading with St Eustatia and St Martins in the Dutch West Indies from 1777 until 1780. [NRS.CS96.3829]

BELL, of Carruthers, WILLIAM, in Falmouth, Jamaica, brother and heir of Thomas Bell in Carruthers in Dumfries-shire. 28 November 1818. [NRS.S/H]

BELL, WILLIAM, in Jamaica, later in Lockerbie, Jamaica, nephew and heir of William Bell in Falmouth, Jamaica, 29 September 1827. [NRS.S/H]

BENNETT, GEORGE WILLIAM, a merchant in Antigua, brother and heir of James Henry Bennett an engineer in Leith who died on 11 April 1874, 9 May 1876, [NRS.S/H]; a sasine, 17 November 1908. [NRS.RS.North Berwick, 20/46]

BENTLEY [?], GEORGE, master of the Walter of Glasgow arrived in Port Glasgow from the West Indies in September 1683. [NRS.E72.19.8]

BERKLEY, ALEXANDER HENRY HASTINGS, born 1825, second son of General Sir George Berkley, died in Mexico on 8 June 1854. [IA]

BERTRAM, JOHN, in Tobago, and his brother William Bertram of Nisbet, an account dated 1777. [NRS.GD5.460]

BERWICK, ELIZABETH, widow of William Brown, and Mary Berwick, in Cumberland Street, Glasgow, daughters and heirs of Newall Berwick in Jamaica, 12 March 1860. [NRS.S/H]

BETHUNE, JOHN, born 2 October 1774 in Alness, Easter Ross, second son of Reverend John Bethune and his wife Catherine Munro, died in Berbice on 18 April 1819. [SM.66.885][F.7.27]

BEVERIDGE, HENRY, born 1798, son of Michael Beveridge the Customs Collector in Kirkcaldy, Fife, died in Demerara on 17 November 1819. [BM.7.231]

BINNEY, ALEXANDER, in St Phillip's parish in Barbados in 1680. [TNA.CO1.44/47]

BIRRELL, GEORGE, a manufactioner in Dunfermline, brother and heir of William Birrell, MD, in Barbados who died on 18 July 1849, 7 June 1850. [NRS.S/H]

BLACK, ANDREW, in Westmoreland, Jamaica, son and heir of Archibald Black a merchant tailor in Glasgow, 26 July 1782, [NRS.S/H]

BLACK, CUTHBERT, took the Association Oath in Antigua in 1696. [TNA]

BLACK, ELIZA, daughter of Peter Black in Kinghorn, Fife, and wife of John Stiven, died on St Thomas in the West Indies on 2 June 1868. [PJ]

BLAIN, Captain, master of the *Mary* from the Clyde to Jamaica in 1795. [NRS.AC7.67]

BLAIR, DUGALD, from Antigua, graduated MD from Glasgow University in 1839. [RGG]

BLAIR, JOHN, born 26 February 1741 in Brechin, Angus, son of Reverend David Blair and his wife Christian Doig, settled in Providence, Essequibo. [F.5.376]

BLAIR, LAMBERT, a planter in Demerara in 1790s. [NRS]

BOGLE, ROBERT, of Shettleston in Glasgow, trading with Demerara in 1795. [NRS.CS96.3201]

BOGUE, JAMES, born 1623 in Edinburgh, enlisted in the Dutch West India Company to Brazil in 1641, married Elizabeth Trail in Tobago, served in Angola, a deed dated 1656. [GAA.NA.1281/167; 1291/161; 1306/214

BONELL, JAMES, from the West Indies, graduated MD from Glasgow University in 1838. [RGG]

BOXILL, WILLIAM, from Barbados, a student at Marischal College in Aberdeen in 1803. [MCA]

BOYD, JOHN, of Mairton Hall in Galloway, died in Bridgetown, Barbados, on 27 June 1798. [AJ]

BOYD, WILLIAM, born 1781, son of Thomas Boyd in Kilmarnock in Jamaica, died in Demerara on 11 May 1804. [SM.66.644]

BOYLE, AGNES, widow of John Key, a tailor in St Eustatia in the Dutch West Indies, 1782. [NRS.CS96.CS17.1.1/28]

BOYLE, JAMES, eldest son of John Boyle a surgeon in St Eustatia, and Agnes Boyle, wife of John Key a tailor in St Eustatia in 1781. [NRS.CS16.1.183]

BOYLE, WILLIAM, master of the Marjory from Bo'ness [?] to Jamaica by 1734. [NRS.HCAS.AC10.194]

BRABNER, Judge, purchased land in Antigua in 1765. [NRS.GD1.32.38.27]

BRAND, JAMES, from Aberdeen, a house-carpenter in Carriacou in the Grenadines, died in 1776. [PSAS.114.494]

BREBNER SINCLAIR and Company, merchants in Glasgow, trading with Surinam and St Eustatia between 1778 and 1782. [NRS.CS96.1413.14]

BREMNER, SOPHIA, youngest daughter of William Bremner in Dominica, was drowned in the wreck of the steamer Duke of Sutherland in Aberdeen Bay on 1 April 1853. [IA]

BRICHAN, JAMES, born 1767, son of George Brichan [1726-1785] and his wife Jean Anderson [1727-1772] in Gallowhill, died in Demerara on 9 August 1802. [Cargill gravestone, Perthshire]

BRODIE, ALEXANDER, born 1738, son of Alexander Brodie of Windyhills in Moray, and his wife Ann Dawson, a merchant in Windyhills, St Mary's parish in Antigua, married Ann Kidder, born 1730, died 1801, in 1766, died on Antigua in 1800. [Caribbeana.1.98]

BRODIE, FRANCIS, a sailor from Windyhills, Moray, died aboard the Unicorn at Darien, Panama, in 1698, testament 1707, Comm. Edinburgh. [NRS]

BROWN, ALEXANDER, a merchant and manufacturer in Arbroath, Angus, trading with St Croix in the Danish West Indies in 1819-1810. [NRS.CS96.828]

BROWN, ANDREW, a sailor from Strichen, Aberdeenshire, died aboard the St Andrew at Darien, Panama, in 1698, testament 1707, Comm. Edinburgh. [NRS.GD406.1.bundle 159/4/18]

BROWN, DAVID, master of the Aldie, from Dundee to Grenada in December 1776. [NRS.E504.11.9]

BROWN, Dr GORDON, born 2 July 1784 son of Reverend Alexander Brown of New Spynie in Moray, died in Demerara in 1813. [EA.5192.13][MCA]

BROWNE, JAMES, in St Lucy's, Barbados, in 1679. [TNA.CO1.44/47]

BROWN, MARGARET, daughter of Reverend Ebenezer Brown in Inverkeithing in Fife, died in Port Maria, Jamaica, on 3 December 1841. [FH]

BROWN, PRICE CARFRAE, fourth son of Charles Brown a merchant in Jamaica, graduated MD from Glasgow University in 1832. [RGG]

BROWNE, THOMAS, a Captain of the 59th Regiment, a letter from Surinam with a sketch of the River Surinam and Fort Zealandia, dated 1799. [NRS.GD51.1.547]

BROWN, WALTER, in Exuma in the Bahama Islands, subscribed to a deed re his wife Elizabeth Walker, in Edinburgh on 1 September 1801. [NRS.RD5.48.399]

BRUCE, ROBERT, master of the Brilliant of Aberdeen from Aberdeen to Grenada, St Kitts, and Tortula in January 1761. [AJ]

BRUCE, WILLIAM, a sailor from Peterhead, Aberdeenshire, died aboard the St Andrew at Darien, Panama, in 1698, testament 1707, Comm. Edinburgh. [NRS]

BRYCE, NINIAN, a shipmaster in Glasgow, a witness in Jamaica in 1750. [NRS.CC8.8.113]

BUCHAN, ALEXANDER, born 1747, died in Grenada on 5 May 1795. [Ramshorn gravestone, Glasgow].

BUCHANAN and SIMPSON, tobacco merchants in Glasgow trading with Jamaica, St Kitts, Antigua and Guadalupe, a letter book from 1759 until 1761. [NRS.CS96.507]

BURNETT, THEODOSIUS, late of Dominica, referred to in the will of John Burnett, a merchant in Aberdeen, before 1784. [NRS.GD23.3.51]

BUSHELL, EDWARD, master of the Two Brothers from Knockfergus in County Antrim, or Port Patrick in Wigtownshire, with 220 Scottish prisoners of war, bound for Jamaica in 1651. [TBNA.SP53.23.75]

BUCHANAN, ALEXANDER, from Tobago, lately in Campbelltown, Argyll, a petition by his trustees dated 22 November 1811. [NRS.CC2.7.59.6]

BUCHANAN, ARTHUR, born 1820, son of Colin Buchanan in Barbados, was educated at Edinburgh Academy from 1828 to 1829. [EAR]

BUCHANAN, COLIN HUGH DALRYMPLE, born 1798, died in Barbados on 24 July 1845. [St Lucy's gravestone]

BUCHANAN, COLIN, born 1818, son of Colin Buchanan in Barbados, was educated at Edinburgh Academy from 1828 to 1829. [EAR]

BUCHANAN, CUMBERLAND, of Fellowship Hall, St Mary's, Jamaica, later in Glasgow by 1808, testament, 1813, Glasgow. [NRS.CS228.B15.52]

BUCHANAN, JOHN, son of the late John Buchanan in Auchentoshan, Dunbartonshire, married Rosa Henrietta Jenken D, of Zacatecas, Mexico, in the British Consulate in Mexico on 4 March 1865. [GM.ns.52.18.778]

BUCHANAN and SIMPSON, tobacco merchants in Glasgow trading with Jamaica, St Kitts, Antigua and Guadalupe, a letter book from 1759 until 1761. [NRS.CS96.507]

BURNETT, THEODOSIUS, late of Dominica, referred to in the will of John Burnett, a merchant in Aberdeen, before 1784. [NRS.GD23.3.51]

BUSHELL, EDWARD, master of the Two Brothers from Knockfergus in County Antrim, or Port Patrick in Wigtownshire, with 220 Scottish prisoners of war, bound for Jamaica in 1651. [TBNA.SP53.23.75

BUDGE, Mrs SARAH WILLIAMS FOWLER, daughter of John Fowler of Trelawney, Jamaica, and widow of Lieutenant George Budge of the Ross-shire Militia, died in June 1816. [NRS.PS3.16.281]

BURGESS, JAMES, in Demerara and Esseqibo, son and heir of William Burgess in Rothes in Moray who died in November 1831. [NRS.S/H]

BURNS, PATRICK, Auditor General of the Leeward Islands, born in February 1807, died on 2 July 1875. [St Andrews Cathedral gravestone, Fife]

CALDER, ARCHIBALD, the Commissary of Stores in Antigua, was admitted as a burgess of Banff in 1768. [BBR]

CALHOUN, JOHN, and Company, merchants in Glasgow, owners of the Neptune of Glasgow, master James Maxwell, trading in linen and cotton with Boston in 1728. [NRS.CS96.3814]; bound from Glasgow to Rotterdam to load goods to exchange for slaves on the coast of Guinea, then via Cork to Africa to acquire slaves, gold dust and elephant teeth, then from Guinea to the Leeward Islands or Barbados or Jamaica to dispose of the slaves and to purchase sugar and cotton before returning to Scotland. Captain James Maxwell died off the Coast of Guinea in 1731. [NRS.CS228.A.3.19]

CAMERON, ANNE, wife of Dr Donald Cameron, a physician in St Thomas, Jamaica, testament, 17 December 1792, Comm. Aberdeen. [NRS]

CAMERON ANN, born 1774, daughter of Alexander Cameron in Invermalie, Lochaber, and relict of James Munro in Surinam, died at Gordonville Place, Inverness, on 20 October 1854. [IA]

CAMERON ANGUS, born 1764, son of Alexander Cameron in Invermalie, died at Paramarido, Surinam, on 3 August 1854. [IA]

CAMERON, CHARLES, Governor of the Bahamas, letters from 1804 until 1819. [NRS.GD51.1.589-591]

CAMERON, DUGALD, a merchant grocer in Greenock, trading with Montreal and Demerara from 1825 until 1831. [NRS.CS96.866]

CAMERON, D. C. and Company, in Berbice from 1816 to 1824. [NRS.CS96.972]

CAMERON, JOHN, a merchant in Berbice deeds from 1817 until 1820. [NRS.RD5.124.257; RD5.191.483]

CAMERON, LEWIS, in Demerara in 1810. [NRS.GD23.10.667]

CAMPBELL, ALEXANDER, formerly in Tobago, settled in Campbeltown, Argyll, by 1796. [NRS.AC7.69]

CAMPBELL, ARCHIBALD, Lieutenant Governor of Jamaica, a letter to Allan Ramsay dated 24 June 1780. [EUL.Campbell of Invernell pp]

CAMPBELL, ARCHIBALD, in Surinam, documents around 1802. [NRS.RH4.196.3]

CAMPBELL, COLIN, master of the Beckie of Greenock trading with Jamaica in 1769. [NRS.E504.15.17]

CAMPBELL, COLIN, from Demerara, married Mary Rose, in Edinburgh on 10 July 1821. [EA.6032.183]

CAMPBELL, COLIN, of the Good Success Plantation, in Essequibo, died in Georgetown, Demerara, on 29 September 1822. [SM.91.128]

CAMPBELL, COLIN, a merchant in Surinam, a deed dated 15 February 1837. [NRS.GD64.Sec.1/320]

CAMPBELL, DOUGALD, master of the Jamaica of Greenock trading with Jamaica in 1772. [NRS.E504.15.22]

CAMPBELL, HEW, a seaman aboard the Walter of Glasgow bound via Port Patrick to the West Indies in January 1683. [NRS.E72.19.8]

CAMPBELL, HUGH, in St Lucy's, Barbados, in 1679. [TNA.CO1.44/47]

CAMPBELL, JAMES, in St Joseph's, Barbados, father of Jennett who was baptised there 1678. [TNA.CO1.44/47]

CAMPBELL, JAMES, a merchant in St George's, Grenada, in 1782. [NRS.HCAS.AC7.58]

CAMPBELL, JAMES, a planter in Tobago, later in Rothesay, Bute, an Edict of Executry dated 12 March 1784. [NRS.CC12.7.24.7]

CAMPBELL, JOHN, a merchant in St Croix, Danish West Indies, later in Greenock, Renfrewshire, testament,1769, Comm. Glasgow. [NRS]

CAMPBELL, JOHN, jr., a merchant in St Ann's, Jamaica, died by 1799. [NRS,AC7.70]

CAMPBELL, JOHN, son of Patrick Campbell of the Royal Bank of Scotland in Edinburgh, died in Berbice on 10 December 1805. [SM.68.78][EEC.1806]

CAMPBELL, JOHN, a merchant in Trinidad, deceased, see deeds 1836-1837. [NRS.GD64.Sec.1.320]

CAMPBELL, Reverend JOHN, in Edinburgh, late from Jamaica, a will, dated 23 April 1878. [NRS.1848.339.52]

CAMPBELL, NEIL, master of the Jamaica of Greenock trading with Jamaica in 1769, later of the Alexander of Greenock trading with Jamaica, in 1772. [NRS.E504.15.73]

CAMPBELL, NEIL, master of the Jessie from Glasgow via Cork bound for Jamaica but was captured by a privateer before 1787. [NRS.AC7.62]

CAMPBELL, THOMAS, in Grenada, died in Demerara in 1795. [SM.57.359]

CAMPBELL, THOMAS, from Inverawe in Argyll, a planter in Demerara in 1798. [RSSP.104]

CAMPBELL, WILLIAM, a sailor, bound for Barbados in November 1667. [Dunbarton Burgess Roll.9]

CAMPBELL, WILLIAM, born in 1727 in Kirkinner, Wigtownshire, son of Reverend Campbell and his wife Margaret Reid, a physician in Antigua who died in 1798. [F.2.365]

CARFRAE, JOHN, a book-seller and stationer in Edinburgh, was appointed facto locentis of John Carfrae in Demerara in 1839. [NRS.CS46.1839.7.205]

CARGILL, RICHARD, Colonel of Militia in St Thomas, Jamaica, in 1776. [IRO][TNA.WO]

CARMICHAEL, H. L., Major General and Acting Governor, died in Demerara in 1813. [EA.5175.13]

CARMICHAEL, THOMAS, born 1757, son of Archibald Carmichael and his wife Frances Applewhite, died 11 April 1789. [St George gravestone, Barbados]

CARR, WILLIAM TAIT, son of James Tait late a merchant in Jamaica, was educated at Marischal College in Aberdeen, graduated MB in 1851, a surgeon in the Royal Navy. [MCA]

CARRILLO, FRANCIS, from Mexico, graduated MD from Glasgow University in 1842. [RGG]

CARRUTHERS, JOHN, settled in Antigua, died in 1700. Probate Prerogative Court of Canterbury. [TNA]   70

CARSTAIRS, W. A., a Member of the Supreme Court, died in Surinam on 1 November 1821. [EEC.17244][S.161][BM.40.263]

CATHCART, FREDERICK, second son of William Cathcart, Earl of Cathcart, married Jean McAdam of Craigengillan, in Berbice on 18 October 1822. [EEC.18113]

CATTENACH, PETER, born 1821 in Kingussie, Inverness-shire, died in Georgetown, Demerara, on 4 April 1853. [IA]

CHALMERS, WILLIAM, son of John Chalmers of Westfield, died in Dominica on 5 July 1811. [AJ]

CHAPMAN, JAMES, from Barbados, graduated MD from Glasgow University in 1839. [RGG]

CHEAP, PATRICK, master of the Loyalty of Glasgow from Glasgow bound for Guinea and Barbados before 1721, was captured by pirates on the return voyage. [NRS.AC9.769]

CHISHOLM, ALEXANDER, son of Provost William Chisholm of Inverness, died on Friendship Plantation in Demerara on 16 July 1799. [GC.1190]

CHISHOLM, BAILLIE, son of John Chisholm in Tullich, Kilmuir, Easter, Ross-shire, died in Plantation Smithfield in Berbice on 4 September 1850. [IA]

CHISHOLM, JAMES FRASER, born 1799, eldest son of Captain Hugh Fraser Chisholm in Fort Augustus, Inverness-shire, died on Plantation, Demerara, on 26 September 1822. [SM..91.127]

CHISHOLM, JOHN, master of the Countess of Kelly of Pittenweem arrived in Anstruther in Fife on 29 May 1767 from New Providence in the Bahamas. [NRS.E504.3.4]

CHISHOLM, ..., mater of the Kingston, arrived in Greenock on 12 August 1749 with a cargo of sugar from St Kitts [AJ]; master of the Isabella from

Greenock to St Kitts with a cargo of bale goods and herring in February 1758. [AJ]

CHRISTIE, JOHN, born in Milntown, Parkhill, Ross-shire, a shipmaster based in St Vincent, died in Kingston, St Vincent, on 25 July 1851. [IA]

CHRISTIE, WILLIAM, in St Phillip's parish in Barbados in 1680. [TNA.CO1.44/47]

CLAPHAM, JAMES, purchased land in Antigua in 1765. [NRS.GD1.32.38.27]

CLARK, DAVID, born 1858, son of Andrew Clark in Kirkcaldy, Fife, died in Georgetown, British Guiana, on 6 April 1885. [PJ]

CLARK, ..., master of the Nancy of Glasgow, arrived in Lancaster from Montserrat in September 1752. [AJ]

CLARKSON, THOMAS, purchased land in Montserrat in 1765. [NRS.GD1.32.38.27]

CLELAND, WILLIAM, took the Association Oath in Barbados on 4 May 1696. [TNA]

CLERK, JAMES, from Jamaica, a Fellow of the Royal College of Surgeons in Edinburgh, in 1792, a Fellow of the Royal College of Physicians in Edinburgh, in 1817, graduated MD at Marischal College, Aberdeen, on 7 February 1817. [MCA]

COCHRANE, JOHN, took the Association Oath in Montserrat in 1696. [TNA]

COCHRAN, JOHN, a cotton yard merchant in Glasgow, trading with Honduras, Mexico, and New York between 1828 and 1831. [NRS.CS96.690.1/2]

COCKBURN, Reverend HENRY, from Kennoway in Fife, died in Grenada on 19 July 1854. [FH]

COCKBURN, Sir WILLIAM JAMES, a report on the evacuation from Banica in Dominica, also a copy of general orders given at Port au Prince, dated 12 April 1797. [NRS.GD216.205]

COGLE, DAVID, a sailor from Wick, Caithness, died aboard the Unicorn at Darien in 1698, testament 1707, Comm. Edinburgh. [NRS]

COLHOUN, ROBERT, in St Kitts, a letter to William McDowal of Castle Semple in 1757. [NRS.GD237.12.47]

COLLY, FRANCIS, was baptised on 7 August 1748, son of James Colly in the Mill of Kennarty, Peterculter, Aberdeenshire emigrated in 1770, a builder and architect who died in St John, Antigua on 26 November 1781. [ANQ]

COLQUHOUN and RITCHIE, merchants in Glasgow, trading with St John, Quebec, Wilmington, Virginia, Antigua, Jamaica, North Carolina and Grenada, between 1791 and 1809. [NRS.CS96.3994]

COMINS, ROBERT, in St Joseph's, Barbados, in 1680. [TNA.CO1.44/47]

CONINGHAM, GEORGE, in St Joseph's, Barbados, in 1680. [TNA.CO1.44/47]

COOPER, Mrs HENRY, lately in St Kitts, now in Irvine, Ayrshire, granted power of attorney to Henry Cooper, a merchant in St Croix in 1795. [NRS.GD23.5.253]

COOPER, WILLIAM, a merchant in Edinburgh, trading with Demerara and Jamaica from 1810 to 1812. [NRS.CS96.687]

COPLAND, ALEXANDER, born 1794 son of William Copland an advocate in Aberdeen, a surgeon in Jamaica, died in Aberdeen on 7 April 1818. [AJ]

COPLAND, GEORGE, a student at Marischal College in Aberdeen around 1803, son of William Copland in Jamaica. [MCA]

COPPEL, ..., master of the Methven of Glasgow, a slaver, bound via Rotterdam and Liverpool for the Windward Coast of Guinea in 1751. [AJ]

CORNFOOT, ANDREW JAMES, born 1807 in Largo in Fife, died at Burnside in Surinam in 1830. [BM.28.574]

CORSTORPHAN, CHARLES, son of Thomas Corstorphine and his wife Ann Johnston, died in Georgetown, Demerara, on 12 August 1867. [St Andrews Cathedral gravestone, Fife]

CORSTORPHAN, GEORGE, born 1806, son of Thomas Corstorphan and his wife Ann Johnston, died in Barbados on 20 September 1834. [St Andrews Cathedral gravestone]

COULTER, Captain, master of the Finlay from Barbados with a cargo of sugar and rum to Greenock, arrived in November 1757. [AJ]

COUPLAND, JOHN, in Martinique, a letter dated 1 August 1795. [NRS.GD51.1.652]

COUSTON, DAVID, master of the Mary was bound from Leith with passengers for Barbados in May 1663 [EBR]

COUTTS, JOHN, master of the Laurel of Aberdeen from Aberdeen to Jamaica in April 1752; master of the Augustus Caesar of Aberdeen, from Aberdeen to Kingston, Jamaica, in June 1753. [AJ]

CRACKE, GEORGE, master of the Janet and Ann of Aberdeen in Grenada in June 1771. [NRS.RD3.238.2/23]

CRAIG, MILLIKEN, of Ballewan, formerly a Commander of the Honourable East India Company Service, died in Demerara on 1 January 1820. [BM.7.119]

CRAIG, WILLIAM, a sailor from Orkney, died aboard the St Andrew at Darien, Panama, in 1698, testament 1707, Comm. Edinburgh. [NRS]

CRAWFORD, ALEXANDER, took the Association Oath in Nevis in 1696. [TNA]

CRAWFORD, DAVID, a merchant in Curacao, Dutch West Indies, before 1773. [NRS.RD4.213.1232]

CRAWFORD, Dr JAMES, in Port Royal, Jamaica, in 1710. [NRS.HCAS.1C7.17.825]

CRAWFORD, ROBERT, a merchant on St Kitts in 1784. [NRS.HCAS.AC7.61]

CRAWFORD, WILLIAM, in St Phillip's parish in Barbados in 1680.] [TNA.CO1.44/47]

CRICHTON, DAVID, son of David Crichton a merchant in Dalkeith, Midlothian, died in Demerara on 25 October 1802. [EA.4074.03] [NRS.CS314.349A]

CROAL, PETER ROSS, from Demerara, graduated MD from Glasgow University in 1837. [RGG]

CROMBIE, FRANCIS, from Edinburgh, died in Demerara on 24 April 1807. [SM.69.638]

CROOKE, JOHN, purchased land in St Kitts and St Eustatia in 1765. [NRS.GD1.32.38.27]

CROPPER, ROBERT P., son of Edward Cropper late a merchant on St Vincent, graduated MA from Marichal College in Aberdeen in 1846. [MCA]

CRUIKSHANK, ALEXANDER, eldest son of Dr Cruikshank in the Haughs of Corsie in Aberdeenshire, died in Nickerie, Surinam, on 13 September 1820. [SM.86.383]

CRUIKSHANK, JAMES, an indentures servant bound for Carriacou near Grenada, in 1804. [PSAS.114.499]

CUMINE, THOMAS JONES, fourth son of Archibald Cumine of Auchry, Aberdeenshire, died in Demerara on 8 February 1820. [BM.7.231]

CUMMINE, WILLIAM, a student at Marischal College in Aberdeen around 1819, son of William Cummine in Jamaica. [MCA]

CUMMING, JAMES, in Carriacou by Grenada, a testament, 3 July 1799, Comm. Edinburgh. [NRS]

CUMMING, LACHLAN, from Moray, a planter in Dutch Demerara by 1791. [Essequibo and Demerara Royal Gazette, 8 April 1812]

CUMMINGS, THOMAS, in St Lucy's, Barbados, in 1679. [TNA.CO1.44/47]

CUMMING, THOMAS, in Demerara in 1779. [NRS.RD4.235.748]; married Isabella Fraser, eldest daughter of Colonel Fraser of Culladrum, there on 6 September 1798. [EA.3622.175]; from Demerara later in Elgin, Moray, a trust disposition dated 23 November 1789, and a testament dated 25 March 1813. [NRS.GD23.10.639/689]; late in Demerara, now in Elgin, a letter to Thomas Newburn in Demerara dated in 1799. [NRS.GD23.6.364]

CUMMING, THOMAS, born 1740 in Dallas, Moray, settled in Demerara as sugar and coffee planter, founded Stabroek, a politician there, died in 1815. [Dallas gravestone] [RSSP.103] [NRS.CO1.44.47]

CUNNINGHAM, ROBERT, a sugar planter on St Kitts took the Association Oath in 1696. [TNA]

CUNNINGHAM, General, Governor of Barbados, letters from Admiral Rodney on the campaign against the French in the West Indies from 1780 to 1782. [NRS.GD18.4216]

CURRIE, ALEXANDER, from Linlithgow, in West Lothian, a merchant in Curacao, Dutch West Indies, died on 15 April 1728, testament, Commissariat of Edinburgh 1 June 1741. [NRS]

CUSHNIE, ARTHUR, a student at Marischal College in Aberdeen about 1803, son of Alexander Cushnie the minister at Oyne in Aberdeenshire, later a merchant in Trinidad. [MCA]

CUTHBERT, G., in Jamaica, a letter to .... Fotheringham dated 19 June 1785. [NRS.GD121.3.80]

DALHOUSIE, Lord, in Martinique, letters to Lady Elizabeth Moncreiff in 1795 to 1796. [NRS.GD45.14.502]

DALL, ALEXANDER CASTLES, born 1815, son of James Dall, died 1850, and Agnes Black died 1869, emigrated in September 1839, of HM Customs in Falmouth, Jamaica, on 8 September 1840. [Cupar gravestone, Fife]

DALLING, JAMES, master of the Anne of Inverness from Inverness via Cork to Barbados in 1716. [NRS.HCAS.AC9/702]

DALLING, RICHARD, master of the Hope of Bo'ness from Leith to Darien in Panama in 1699. [NRS.GD406]

DALMAHOY, JOHN, son of Dr Dalmahoy in Jamaica, was educated at Edinburgh Academy from 1826 to 1828. [EAR]

DALZELL, COUTTS TROTTER, third son of Alexander Dalzell, died in Demerara on 31 December 1818. [BM.3.246]

DASHWOOD, Colonel CHARLES, in Xalapa. Mexico, a letter to Lieutenant Colonel Mercer, dated 27 January 1828. [NRS.GD172.1185]

DAUNEY, WILLIAM JOHN, a student at Marischal College in Aberdeen, in 1851, son of William Dauney a lawyer in Demerara. [MCA]

DAVIDSON, ALEXANDER, a grocer in Edinburgh, trading with Demerara before 1808. [NRS.CS96.671]

DAVIDSON, CHARLES, son of John Davidson of Tillichetly in Aberdeenshire, was educated at King's College in Aberdeen from 1790 until

1794, a physician in St George's, Grenada, died there on 2 October 1804. [KCA][AJ]

DAVIDSON, JAMES, in Jamaica, Power of Attorney to Alexander Woodburn, dated 24 August 1838. [NRS.RD5.1136.269/119]

DAVIDSON, JANE, from Surinam to Jamaica on the America in June 1675. [SPAWI.1675.285]

DAVIDSON, JOHN, in Aberdeen, formerly in exile in Barbados, returned and was admitted as a burgess of Aberdeen on 14 November 1666. [ABR]

DAVIDSON, WILLIAM, from Surinam to Jamaica on the America in June 1675. [SPAWI.1675.285]

DAVIS, JOHN, purchased land in Antigua in 1765. [NRS.GD1.32.38.27]

DAWSON, CHARLES, MD, surgeon of the 54th Regiment, died of yellow fever in Antigua on 13 November 1849. [IA]

DEAN, JAMES, born 1823, son of James Dean the parochial teacher in Rothes, Moray, died on Stonevastigheld Plantation in Berbice on 16 November 1853. [IA]

DEMPSTER, ALEXANDER, seventh son of James Dempster a surgeon in Cupar, Fife, died on Dunkley's Estate, Vere, Jamaica on 24 October 1835. [FH]

DEMPSTER, Dr ANTHONY, son of James Dempster a surgeon in Cupar, Fife, died in Manchester, Jamaica in Septeber 1847. [FH]

DEMPSTER, Dr DAVID, fifth son of James Dempster a surgeon in Cupar, Fife, died in Spanish Town, Jamaica on 3 December 1834. [FJ]

DEWAR, GEORGE, born 1835, son of James Dewar in Aberdour in Fife, died at Goldstone Hall in Berbice on 1 February 1875. [FH]

DEWAR, WILLIAM, son of James Dewar in Aberdour in Fife, died at Hope and Experiment Plantation in Demerara on1 December 1865. [FH]

DICKSON, JOHN, son of Gilbert Dickson in Glasgow, died in Demerara on 6 December 1808. [SM.71.238]

DONALDSON, ROBERT, took the Association Oath in Antigua in 1696. [TNA]

DOUGLAS, COLIN, died in Demerara on 27 December 1827. [EA.6615.255]

DOUGLAS, GILBERT, of Douglas Park, a planter at Fairfield, Demerara, from 1801 until 1807. [NRS.CS96.4901]

DOUGLAS, JAMES, from Springwood Park, Kelso, Roxburghshire, a planter at Weiburg on the River Demerara, by 1762. [RSSP.102]

DOUGLAS, JAMES SHOLTO, an Ensign of the 50th [Queen's Own] Regiment, stationed in Jamaica around 1776. [TNA.WO][IRO]

DOUGLAS, JAMES, second son of James Douglas, an accountant in Edinburgh, died in Paramaribo, Surinam, on 7 November 1874. [S.9785]

DOUGLAS, JOHN, master of the Molly of Glasgow was bound for St Kitts in 1761. [NRS.AC7.50]

DOUGLAS, JOHN, master of the brig Sally of Kirkcaldy in Fife, subscribed to a Bill of Exchange, in Kingston, Jamaica, on 12 March 1796, drawn on John McDonnell a merchant in Dublin. [NRS.AC7.72]

DOUGLAS, ROBERT, a sugar planter at Better Hope in Demerara, died in Edinburgh on 5 April 1826. [BM.19.766]

DOVE, WILLIAM, in Jamaica around 1815, son of John Dove of Pargillies in Fife, a deed. [NRS.B34/8/1; B34.15.9-10]

DOW, Captain ROBERT RAMSAY, son of J. B. Dow in Leith, died in Honduras in 1853. [EEC.22500]

DRUMMOND, DAVID, a mariner from Kirkwall, Orkney, aboard the Vito Galley in 1701. [Barbados Archives. RB6.43.269]

DRUMMOND, GEORGE, from Orkney, surgeon aboard the Blessing in Barbados, probate 23 May 1701, Barbados Archives.[RB6.43.269]

DRUMMOND, Dr JOHN, was killed in a duel in Savannah la Mar, Jamaica, on 20 June 1754. [SM.16.600]

DUFF, WILLIAM, from St George in Grenada, was admitted as a burgess of Banff in 1797. [BBR]

DUGUID, GEORGE, born 1783, died on Orangestein Estate in Essequibo, on 7 January 1807. [SM.69.798]

DUNCAN, ARCHIBALD, a merchant in Glasgow trading with Mexico, Cuba, Haiti, Columbia, Montreal and New York in 1830. [NRS.CS96.912.1]

DUNCAN, FRANK, born 13 April 1817, son of Thomas Duncan in Grenada, was educated at Edinburgh Academy from 1825 to 1831. [EAR]

DUNCAN, GEORGE, master of the Happy Return from Scotland with passengers bound for Barbados on 28 September 1698, landed there on 11 December 1698. [NRS.RH15.101.3]

DUNCAN, Mrs ISABEL, wife of William Duncan master of the Scotia of Banff, letters from American and West Indian ports dated from 1884 to 1886. [NRS.NRAS.0919]

DUNCAN, THOMAS, born 1815, son of Thomas Duncan in Grenada, was educated at Edinburgh Academy from 1824 to 1831. [EAR]

DUNCAN, WILLIAM, a merchant in Berbice, died on 21 April 1814. [EC.6211]

DUNCAN, Captain, master of the Diligence of Aberdeen from Aberdeen to Antigua in March 1753. [AJ]

DUNKIN, ANDREW, in St Phillip's parish in Barbados in 1680. [TNA.CO1.44/47]

DUNLOP, ROBERT, a manufacturer and shipowner in Irvine, Ayrshire, trading with Tobago and St Croix in the Danish West Indies, in 1812. [NRS.CS96.2592]

DUNN, JOHN, a merchant and shipowner in Greenock, trading with Jamaica, Bermuda and Cuba from 1820 until 1823. [NRS.CS96.893]

EASDALE, JOHN, master of the Jean of Greenock trading with Jamaica before 1730. [NRS.AC9.1104]

EASSON, ROBERT, master of the Lord Frederick from Greenock to Barbados in December 1764. [NRS.E504.15]

ELLIOT, JOHN, from Tobago, graduated MD from Glasgow University in 1836. [RGG]

ELLIOT, JOHN, a planter in Tobago, versus William McLean formerly in Dumfries, a decreet dated June 1837. [NRS.CS46.1837.6.35]

ELLIOT, MARY, wife of Thomas Elliot, was buried in St Philip's, Barbados, on 20 September 1679. [TNA.CO1.44/7]

ELLIOT, PETER, in St Lucy's, Barbados, in 1679. [TNA.CO1.44/47]

ELLIOT, ROBERT, in St Phillip's parish in Barbados in 1680. [TNA.CO1.44/47]

ELLIOT, ROBERT, in Demerara, 1779. [NRS.RD4.235.748]

ELLIOT, THOMAS, son of Thomas Elliot in Jamaica deceased, a student at King's College, Aberdeen, in 1816. [KCA]

ELLIS, JOHN, a student at Marischal College in Aberdeen, in 1802, son of William Ellis in Jamaica. [MCA]

ELMSLIE, ..., master of the Two Brothers of Fraserburgh in Aberdeenshire, from Antigua bound for Holland in 1751. [AJ]

ETTLES, JOHN, son of Robert Ettles in Inverness, died in Demerara on 26 July 1823. [EA.5199.271]

EWART, ROBERT, in Jamaica, a letter to Adam Ewart, around 1755. [NRS.NRAS.Tweedie-Stoddart of Oliver pp]

EWING. ..., master of the Grizel of Irvine arrived from the West Indies in February 1752. [AJ]

FAIRBAIRN, FRANCIS MACKENZIE, son of ... Fairbairn in Berbice, died in Demerara on 24 September 1823. [BM.15.249]

FAIRBAIRN, PETER, died in Berbice on 10 June 1822. [BM.12.519]

FAIRFULL, ALEXANDER S., from St Andrews, in Fife, died in Kingston, Jamaica, on 21 July 1852. [FJ]

FAIRNIE, ALEXANDER, on St Martins in the Dutch West Indies in 1784. [NRS.HCAS.AC7.61]

FALCONER, JAMES C., from Inverness, was educated at King's College in Aberdeen around 1847, later in Jamaica. [KCA]

FARLEY, JAMES HENRY, from Antigua, graduated MD from Glasgow University in 1839. [RGG]

FARRE, JOHN RICHARD, born in Barbados on 31 January 1775, graduated MD at Glasgow University in 1802, later graduated MD at King's College, Aberdeen, in 1806. A medical practitioner in Barbados and in London, he founded the Royal London Ophthalmic Hospital, died on 7 May 1862. [RGG]

FARQUHAR, ALEXANDER, born on 27 October 1761, son of Alexander Farquhar in Kintore in Aberdeenshire, was educated at King's College in Aberdeen around 1781, settled in Antigua. [KCA]

FARQUHARSON, ANDREW, in Demerara in 1796. [NRS.RH1.852]

FARQUHARSON, CHARLES MILLER, born 1815, son of Charles Farquharson in Jamaica, was educated at Edinburgh Academy from 1827 to 1831. [EAR]

FERGUSON, ARTHUR, son of William Ferguson, was buried in St Philip's, Barbados, on 1 April 1679. [TNA.CO1.44/47]

FERGUSON, CHARLES, born in August 1708, son of Reverend Adam Ferguson and his wife Mary Gordon in Crathie, Aberdeenshire, died in Port Royal, Jamaica, on 8 April 1747. [F.4.189]

FERGUSON, DAVID, master of the Swan of Ayr arrived in Ayr on 28 September 1678 from Montserrat and the West Indies. [RRS.E72.3.4]

FERGUSON, JAMES, late from Essequibo, now in Stranraer in 1821. [NRS.CS17.1.40.393]]

FERGUSSON, THOMAS, eldest son of Peter Fergusson in Inch, Wigtownshire, graduated CM from Glasgow University in 1817, a surgeon at St John's, Antigua, died there on 21 May 1845. [RGG]

FIFE, LAURENCE, a student at Marischal College in Aberdeen around 1819, son of Macduff Fife in St. Vincent. [MCA]

FINLAYSON, JOHN, master of the Beattie of Bo'ness, from Greenock to Antigua in 1712. [NRS.HCAS.AC8.139]

FINLAYSON, JOHN HOYES, born 1821, son of Reverend John Finlayson in Cromarty, died in Kingston, Jamaica, on 2 November 1849. [IA]

FLEMING, DAVID, son of George Fleming, died in Edenbank, Demerara, on 23 August 1850. [FH]

FLEMING, THOMAS, from St Andrews, Fife, an engineer died in Georgetown, Demerara, on 4 December 1853. [FH]

FLETCHER, ..., was born in Berbice on 14 December 1805. [SM.68.155]

FORBES, JEAN, born in 1737, daughter of Thomas Forbes of Waterton, and his wife Margaret Montgomerie, married Walter Thibou a physician in Antigua. [FF]

FORBES, JOHN, born 20 December 1767, son of James Forbes and his wife Sarah Gordon in Gamrie, Banffshire, a merchant in the Bahamas, probate 2 October 1820, Mobile. [Will book 1]

FORBES, WILLIAM, son of Margaret Anderson in Aberdeen, a vintner in St Michael's parish in Barbados, probate 24 October 1718, Barbados. [RB6.4.388]

FORTUNE, ALEXANDER, son of Dr John Fortune in Grenada, died in Melbourne, Australia, on 28 January 1854. [FH]

FORTUNE, JOHN, son of John Fortune in Grenada, was educated at Marichal College in Aberdeen around 1841. [MCA]

FORTUNE JOHN, son of John Fortune and his wife Margaret Gray, died in Kingston, Jamaica, on 1 October 1853. [St Andrews Cathedral gravestone, Fife]

FOULIS, PETER, born 1836, son of Robert Foulis gardener at Fordell [died 1877] an engineer of the Royal Navy, died in Bermuda on 31 October 1875. [FH]

FRASER, ALEXANDER, in Tobago, testament dated 30 August 1784, brother of Major James Fraser of Belladrum. [NRS.GD23.10.594/608]

FRASER, GEORGE, born in Sutherland, formerly in Ceylon, died at Richmond Hill, in Grenada, on 10 September 1855. [IA]

FRASER, HUGH, born 1820, died in St Vincent on 31 July 1855. [IA]

FRASER, JAMES, the younger of Belladrum in Inverness-shire, a planter in Demerara from 1790. [NRS.HCA; D238/D1.17.6]

FRASER, JAMES, of Belladrum in Inverness-shire, appointed his son James Fraser in Demerara and George Inglis, a planter in Demerara, as his attorneys in Demerara and Berbice in Dutch Guyana in 1795. [NRS.GD23.5.352]

FRASER, JAMES, of Belladrum in Guyana, a planter in Berbice by 1801. [NRS.GD46.17] [RSSP.105]

FRASER, JAMES, from Pitcalzean in Ross-shire, a planter in Berbice before 1801. [RSSP.105]; probate 15 August 1801, Prerogative Court of Canterbury. [TNA]

FRASER, JAMES, born 1855 son of William Fraser a butler in Pitmilly, a draper in Cupar, died in Georgetown, DemPJ]erara, on 9 May 1881. [

FRASER, JOHN, a carpenter aboard the Conclusion was captured by the Turks when on a return voyage from Barbados, then imprisoned in Algiers in 1679. [RPCS.VII.152]

FRASER, JOHN, a plantation owner in Dominica, letters from 1800 to 1804. [NRS.AD58-263]

FRASER, JOHN, from Aberdeen, a skipper and merchant who settled in St Kitts, where he died before 1747. [ACA.APB.3.137]

FRASER, SIMON, eldest son of Donald Fraser of Balloan, of the Golden Fleece Plantation in Berbice, died there on 15 September 1803. [DPCA.72]

FRASER, SUSAN, eldest daughter of Simon Fraser of Kilmorack, married M. Katz, in Berbice on 9 January 1826. [EA]

FRASER, THOMAS, in St Vincent, a letter to Simon Fraser, a baker in Inverness, dated 4 January 1790. [HCA.D238.D1.17.6]

FRASER, WILLIAM, a planter in Berbice in 1818. [NRS.CS96.2130.1]

FREDERICI, Governor of Surinam, letters from 1801 to 1803. [NRS.GD46.17.21/15/189]

FRIGG, ANDREW, a skipper in Jamaica, son of John Frigg a merchant in Findhorn in Moray, died in Edinburgh in 1769. [NRS.CC8.8.123]

FRIZELL, DANIEL, father of Ann Frizell who was baptised in St Lucy's, Barbados, on 14 October 1678. [TNA.CO1.44-47]

FRIZALL, JOHN, in St Phillip's parish in Barbados in 1680. [TNA.CO1.44/47]

FULLARTON, GEORGE, took the Association Oath in Montserrat in 1696. [TNA]

FYFE, DAVID, from Dundee, settled on Black River Estate, Jamaica, around 1760. [NLJ.ms655.3]

GALLIE, WILLIAM, from Edinburgh, in Trinidad, a deed dated 24 May 1875. [NRS.RD5.1770.339/197]

GALLOWAY, EDWARD, in St Lucy's, Barbados, in 1679. [TNA.CO1.44/47]

GARDINER, GORDON, a student at Marischal College in Aberdeen around 1817, son of Edwin Gardiner in Trinidad. [MCA]

GARDINER, WILLIAM, a student at Marischal College in Aberdeen around 1817, later was the assistant surgeon of the 56th Regiment of Foot, son of Edwin Gardiner in Trinidad. [MCA]

GARIOCH, ANDREW, master of the Cumberland of Fraserburgh in Aberdeenshire, from Aberdeen to Antigua on 28 February 1747. [NRS.E504.1.2]

GARRETT, GARRETT, master of the brigantine Hanover of Glasgow from Port Glasgow via Guinea to the West Indies and return in 1719. [NRS.HCAS.AC7.433]

GASS, ROBERT, master of the Marigold of Glasgow from Barbados to Greenock in 1691. [NRS.RD3.78.32]

GEDDES, JOHN, born 1829, son of Alexander Geddes [died 1841] and his wife Jean Ramsay [died 1848] in Cupar, Fife, died in Villa, Westmoreland, Jamaica, on 27 August 1857. [FH]

GELLIE, LEWIS, master of the Betsy and Mary of Aberdeen from Aberdeen to Antigua on 16 November 1750, later master of the snow Antigua Packet of Aberdeen bound from Aberdeen to Antigua in 1752. [AJ]

GENTLEMAN, DAVID, master of the Elizabeth of Montrose died in Jamaica by 1719. [NRS.HCAS.AC9.647]

GEORGE, JOHN, son of John George in Willowbank,Wick, Caithness, died in Jamaica on 1 November 1849. [IA]

GERARD, WILLIAM, in New York, a contract with Juan Albarez Vesina, a shipmaster, to ship a cargo from New York to the Caribbean in May 1782. [NRS.GD1.768.13]

GIBBON, WILLIAM, master of the St Andrew of Aberdeen a snow, from Aberdeen bound for Jamaica in June 1758. [AJ]

GIBBS. PHILIP, in St Pierre, Martinique, a letter to the Earl of Leven regarding Vice Admiral Cochrane's and Lord Balgonie's recent gallant behaviour, dated 6 March 1810. [NRS.GD26.9.561]

GIBSON, JAMES, master of the Carolina Merchant from Glasgow to the Caribee Islands on 29 April 1686. [TNA.CO5.287.126]

GIBSON, NINIAN, master of the Jean of Largs from Port Glasgow on 26 April 1684 bound for the West Indies. [NRS.E72.19.9]

GILCHRIST, JOHN, carpenter on board Roger Gale's ship the Benjamin of the Bay of Honduras in 1778. [NRS,HCAS.AC7,58]

GILHAGIE, ..., master of the Janet of Glasgow bound for the West Indies in 1667. [Dean of Guild Court of Glasgow]

GILLESPIE, GEORGE, a merchant in Greenock trading with Jamaica in 1796. [NRS.E504.15.73]

GILLESPIE, JAMES, in Jamaica, a letter to Archibald Grant, dated 7 October 1767. [NRS.GD345.117/1.128]

GIRVAN, THOMAS, an engineer cum contractor from Maybole, Ayrshire, settled in St Thomas in Jamaica, executory papers, [n/d]. [NRS.GD27.7.271]

GLASFORD, ALEXANDER, master of the Jamaica Packet trading between Leith and Jamaica in 1751 and in 1752. [AJ]

GLASGOW, Dr ROBERT, on St Vincent, a letter to William Glasgow dated 4 June 1774. [NRS.NRAS.Hunter of Hunterston pp, bundle 169]

GLENFIELD, ROBERT, master of the Benjamin of Glasgow arrived in Port Glasgow in June 1681 from the West Indies. Returned to the West Indies in July 1681. [NRS.E72.19.1/2]

GLOVER, JOHN, master of the <u>Salmon of Chester</u> trading between Glasgow and Nevis in 1681. [NRS.E72.19.5]

GOLDIE, THOMAS DICKSON, born 1799, son of James Goldie in Bonnyrigg, Midlothian, died in Demerara on 1 December 1820.[BM.8.708]

GOLLIER, JAMES, trading between Ayr and Montserrat in 1642. [NRS.RD1.544.6]

GORDON, ADAM, born on 11 October 1812, son of Reverend William Gordon and his wife Catherine Brodie in Elgin, Moray, died on Richmond Estate, St Vincent, on 23 March 1832. [F.6.391]

GORDON, ALEXANDER, was proposed for the Council of Montserrat in 1765. [SPAWI]

GORDON, ALEXANDER, a planter in Tobago, an executor on 29 January 1801. [NRS.GD44.43.339]

GORDON, ALEXANDER, the elder, in Tobago, versus Charlotte More, daughter of Graham More in Edinburgh, a Process of Divorce dated 1815. [NRS.CC8.6.1580]

GORDON, CHARLES, born 1719 in Aberdeen, a merchant in Jamaica by 1755. [SAA.203; SM.17.514]

GORDON, GEORGE, President of the Court of Justice in Berbice, died there on 13 November 1820. [BM.9.708]

GORDON, JAMES, a merchant on St Kitts by 1767, died there in 1770. [Clatt gravestone, Aberdeenshire][NRS.RGS.109.165]

GORDON, JOHN, Major of the 50th Regiment, stationed in Jamaica around 1776. [TNA.WO][IRO]

GORDON, JOHN, born on 24 March 1782, son of Thomas Gordon in Aboyne, Aberdeenshire, was educated in King's College in Aberdeen from 1795 until 1799, settled in Jamaica. [KCA]

GORDON, JOHN, in Plantation Huntly in Demerara, a letter dated 1811. [NRS.GD23.6.484]

GORDON, JOHN, sr., third son of John Gordon of Balmuir a Writer to the Signet, a Captain of the 2nd [Queen's] Regiment, died in Barbados on 22 December 1816. [AJ]

GORDON, JOHN, born 1821, a planter in Demerara, died on 19 August 1880. [Burntisland gravestone in Fife]

GORDON, PETER, of Plantation Borlum, in Berbice, dead by 1809. [NRS.GD23.7.39; GD23.10.667]

GORDON, ROBERT, a merchant in New Providence in the Bahamas, probate 1723 in the Bahamas.

GORDON, ROBERT, of Hope Estate in Demerara, married Ann Parkinson, in Demerara on 3 June 1804. [SM.66.806]

GORDON, ROBERT, in Barbados, a Letter of Attorney to Umphrey Robertson dated 10 June 1861. [NRS.RD5.1135.387/114]

GORDON, THOMAS, in Jamaica, a letter to Archibald Grant dated 29 July 1753. [NRS.GD345.1162.4.40]

GORDON, THOMAS, born on 1 July 1768, son of Reverend George Gordon and his wife Cecilia Reid in Keith, Banffshire, settled at Overhall, Port Maria Bay, Jamaica, died on passage home on 15 June 1807. [AJ][F.6.321]

GORDON, Dr WILLIAM, second son of John Gordon of Carroll, died in Demerara on 7 January 1817. [S.7.17]

GORDON, WILLIAM, a student at Marischal College in Aberdeen around 1822, son of William Gordon MD in Jamaica. [MCA]

GORRIE, MALCOLM, a letter from William Howatson on the death of Sir John Gorrie, dated 25 August 1892. [NRS.GD1.1441.1Od]

GOURLAY, DAVID, master of the Roselle trading between Leith and Jamaica before 1799. [NRS.AC7.72]

GRACE, PETER, son of Dr Grace in Cupar, Fife, died in Jamaica on 26 April 1824. [FH]

GRAEME, ROBERT, from Garioch, Aberdeenshire, a plantation manager in St Mary's parish, Jamaica, in 1786. [NLS.ms10925.34]

GRAHAM, JAMES, a plantation manager in Hanover parish, Jamaica, in 1786. [NLS.ms10925.34]

GRAHAM, Captain JAMES, born 1623, died in Barbados on 12 July 1730. [St Lucy's gravestone]

GRAHAM, ROBERT, overseer on Melville's estates in Dominica before 1784. [NRS.GD22.2.67]

GRAHAM, ...,master of the Montrose from Greenock with a cargo of bale goods bound for Antigua on 23 September 1749. [AJ]

GRANT, ALEXANDER, in St Croix in the Virgin Islands, a letter to James Grant his attorney in Inverness, dated 18 June 1809. [NRS.GD23 6 459]

GRANT, ALEXANDER, in Plantation Good Intent in Demerara in 1810. [NRS,GD23.10.667]

GRANT, ALLEN, an Ensign of the 60th [Royal American] Regiment in Jamaica in 1776. [TNA.WO][IRO]

GRANT, DAVID, in Jamaica, a letter to Sir Archibald Grant dated 12 November 1760. [NRS.GD345]

GRANT, FRANCIS, a letter to Charles Gordon dated 28 September 1784. [AUL.ms1160.6.34]

GRANT, J., a letter to Sir Alexander Grant re Jamaica and Stork's ship in East Florida, dated 15 November 1769. [NRS.GD1.32.38]

GRANT, JOHN, in St Lucy's, Barbados, in 1679. [TNA.CO1.44/47]

GRANT, JOHN, in Jamaica, a letter to Charles Gordon dated 28 November 1785. [AUL.ms1160.6.36]

GRANT, General LEWIS, at Government House in the Bahamas a letter concerning affairs in the West Indies on 1 June 1824. [NRS.GD45.3.126]

GRANT, LEWIS, a bookseller in Inverness, trading with Demerara from 1824 until 1825. [NRS.CS96.74]

GRANT, MARY JOANNA, only daughter of William V in Demerara, married Robert Tulloch, in Golden Square, Edinburgh, in 1811. [SM.73.398]

GRANT, Sir R. of Dalvey put his estates in Jamaica into the hands of Richard Oswald of Auchencreive, bonds from 1771 until 1893.

GRANT, WALTER, a surgeon and physician in Jamaica, graduated MD from King's College in Aberdeen in 1753. [MCA] ; settled in Jamaica, a letter to Captain Archibald Grant , dated 2 September 1763. [NRS.GD345.1180]

GRANT, WILLIAM, in St Joseph's, Barbados, in 1680. [TNA.CO1.44/47]

GRANT, WILLIAM, of Kilgraston in Perthshire, son of Patrick Grant of Glenlochy [1709-1783], and his wife Beatrice Grant, [1711-1780], Chief Justice of Jamaica from 1783, died in Edinburgh on 29 March 1793. [St Cuthbert's gravestone in Edinburgh] and Kirkmichael's gravestone in Banffshire]

GRANT, WILLIAM, from Strathspey, a planter in Demerara in 1798. [RSSP.104]

GRANT, WILLIAM G. M. in St Vincent, a deed dated 6 July 1847. [NRS.RD5.1117.483/6]

GRAY, ALEXANDER, in Trinidad, a testament dated 10 August 1860. [NRS.RD5.1119.137/14]

GRAY, JAMES, a sailor aboard the Concord bound for Jamaica in 1732. [SL]

GRAY, PATRICK, born 1746, settled on the Friendship Estate, Hanover, Jamaica, died on 24 July 1806 at Glendoick House in Perthshire. [Kinfauns gravestone]

GREEN, JOHN, master of the Helpwell from Portpatrick in Wigtownshire, or Knockfergus in County Antrim, with 300 Scottish prisoners of war bound for Jamaica in 1654. [TNA.SP.77]

GREENFIELD, ROBERT, master of the Benjamin of Glasgow from Port Glasgow to the West Indies on 7 August 1681. [NRS.E72.19.4]

GREIG, ARCHIBALD, master of the Ceres from St Kitts to Greenock in 1779-1780. [NRS.HCAS.AC7.58]

GRIEVE, ARCHIBALD, son of Thomas Grieve a merchant in Edinburgh, died in Kingston, Jamaica, on 26 November 1851. [IA]

GUMONS, JACOB, purchased land in Antigua in 1765. [NRS.GD1.32.38.27]

GUNN, PETER, son of Captain Gunn of the <u>Good Design of Wick,</u> died aboard the <u>Congress</u> when bound for the West Indies on 25 January 1854. [IA]

GUTHRIE, JAMES, the assistant Quarter Master General in Jeremie, Haiti, from 1796 until 1798, later from 1799 to 1801 as a Brigade Major in Canada. [NRS.GD188.28.1]

HADDOW, SCOTT, and DALE, merchants in Glasgow, trading with New York and Demerara from 1819 to 1820. [NRS.CS96.3384]

HALDAN, JOHN, in Edinburgh, versus James Struthers in Demerara, 1828-1829. [NRS.CS96.2045]

HALYBURTON, THOMAS, in St Eustatia, Dutch West Indies, in 1787, [NRS.S/H] dead by 1795, Testament, [NRS.CC8.8.130-131]

HAMILTON, HUGH, a planter in Jamaica, letters with news of naval action against the French in the West Indies from 1779 until 1791. [NRS.GD142.3]

HAMILTON, JOHN, took the Association Oath in Antigua on 14 May 1696. [TNA]

HAMILTON, H., a plantation manager in Hampden parish, Jamaica, in 1786. [NLS.ms10925.34]

HAMILTON, JOHN, took the Association Oath in Antigua on 14 May 1696. [TNA]

HAMILTON, JOHN, and Company, merchants in Greenock, trading with Jamaica and Demerara in 1815 to 1816. [NRS.CS96.2044]

HAMILTON, JOHN, of Sundrum, father of Captain Hugh Hamilton of the 60TH Regiment in St Croix in 1810. [NRS.GD51.6.700]

HAMILTON, ROBERT, in Jamaica, a letter to Thomas Garvine dated 31 August 1740. [GUA. Hamilton of Rozelle pp.3.15]

HAMILTON, W., in Nevis, bound on the expedition to St Bartholemew and to St Martin, in the Dutch West Indies, a letter dated 20 February 1689. [NRS.GD204.1.1205]

HAMILTON, W. took the Association Oath in Nevis in 1696. [TNA]

HARDY, Reverend ROBERT, in Berbice, graduated LL.D. at Glasgow University in 1837. [RGG]

HARDIE, ROBERT, an engineer, died in Surinam on 5 November 1861. [S.2030]

HARPER, BLENEY, in Barbados, a letter to William Gordon and Company in Glasgow, concerning the condition of slaves on the Neptune of Glasgow in May 1731. [NRS.CS228.A.3.19/32]

HARRIS, GEORGE WASHINGTON, superintendent of an estate in St Kitts, afterwards settled in Grenada, graduated BA from Glasgow University in 1844. [RGG]

HARRISON, JOHN, mate aboard the James of Ayr, from Ayr to the West Indies on 5 February 1681, arrived in Ayr on 19 September 1681 from the West Indies, from Ayr to the Caribee Islands on 13 March 1683, arrived in Ayr on 7 September 1683 from Montserrat. [NRS.E72.3.7/11/12]

HARTLEY, RICHARD, master of the St George of Montrose from Montrose in Angus bound for Africa and Antigua in 1754. [NRS.AC7.46.5]

HARVEY, JAMES OCTAVIUS LEE, of Castle Semple, and family, owners of the Conference Sugar Estate in Grenada, from 1817 until 1883. [NRS.GD241.49]

HARVEY, JOHN, a shipmaster, died 15 September 1827, probate, St Jan, Danish West Indies, 1826-1836, folio.25. [RAK]

HARVEY, JOHN and ALEXANDER HARVEY, in Barbados, 1749. [NRS.HCAS.AC9.1866.109]

HATHORN, EBENEZER, master of the Margaret of Leith bound for the West Indies in 1718. [NRS.HCAS.AC9.626]

HAY, DAD, a Customs officer, died in Surinam on 30 October 1807. [SM.70.399]

HAY, ROBERT, master of the Janet of Leith from Leith bound for the West Indies in 1611. [NRS.E71.29.6/Folio 22]

HENDERSON, Captain ARCHIBALD, married Elizabeth Yeamans in St John's, Barbados, on 12 November 1670. [St John's marriage Register]

HENDERSON, THOMAS, in St Lucy's, Barbados, in 1679. [TNA.CO1.44/47]

HENDERSON, WILLIAM, a student at Marischal College in Aberdeen around 1820, son of William Henderson a soldier in Jamaca. [MCA]

HENDERSON, Dr, his children in Jamaica, discharged George Bogle his executor on 24 September 1832. [NRS.RD.469.460.169]

HERDMAN, THOMAS, master of the Harriet from Aberdeen via Madeira, Barbados, Grenada, Antigua, bound for Virginia on 20 February 1767. [AJ]

HERON, GEORGE ROBERT, from Jamaica, graduated MD from Glasgow University in 1843. [RGG]

HERRIES, JOHN, born 24 April 1721 son of Robert Herries of Halldykes and his wife Mary Scroggs, a merchant in India and Jamaica, later settled in Jamaica by 1756, died there in October 1759. [Herries of Halldykes]

HERRIES, WILLIAM, master of the Walter of Glasgow arrived in Port Glasgow from the Caribee Islands in September 1682, again in January 1683. [NRS.E72.19.5/8]

HETHERINGTON, JOHN, an overseer in St Jan, Danish West Indies, died 29 August 1831, probate, St Jan, 1826-1836, fos. 82-112. [RAK]

HILL, WILLIAM, master of the Swallow of Dundee trading between Dundee and Grenada in 1773, also in 1774. [NRS.E504.11.8]

HODGESON, JOHN, master of the Unity of Ayr arrived in Ayr on 2 September 1673 from Montserrat. [NRS.E72.3.3]

HOME, DAVID WILLIAM MILNE, born 1873, son of Colonel David Milne Home [1838-1901], Private Secretary to the Governor of Trinidad, letters from 1888 until 1901, he died in 1918. [NRS.GD267.35.3.9]

HOME, NINIAN, the Lieutenant Governor of Grenada, and owner of the Waltham Plantation there, papers from 1790 until 1840. [NRS.GD267]

HOME, WILLIAM, son of William Home of Broomhouse, an officer in the Royal Marines in the West Indies during the American War, letters from 1778 until 1782 regarding HMS Intrepid and encounters with the French fleet. [NRS.GD1.384.617]

HOOD, MATTHEW, a carpenter in Glasgow, later in St Paul, Tobago, versus Elizabeth Craig, daughter of a collier in Rutherglen, Lanarkshire, who married in 1793, a Process of Divorce dated 2 May 1800. [NRS.CC8.6.1088]

HOPE, Sir JOHN, in the West Indies: a letter concerning the capture of St Lucia, Grenada, and St Vincent, dated 24 Jue 1796, a letter re the capture of Trinidad, dated 20 February 1797, and a letter re the failure to capture Puerto Rica, dated 1May 1797. [NRS.GD364.1.1081]

HOPE, JOHN, a surgeon from Nevis, died in Demerara on 11 August 1804. [SM.66.97]

HORN, JOHN, was aboard the Mayflower of Glasgow when it arrived in Port Glasgow in September 1684 from the West Indies. [NRS.E72.19.9]

HOUSTON, ANDREW, in Grenada, a deed dated 15 May 1828. [NRS.433.591]

HOYES, JOHN, a student at Marischal College in Aberdeen around 1819, son of John Hoyes in Jamaica. [MCA]

HOYES, JOHN, in Edinburgh, late of Jamaica, a Trust Deed dated 18 December 1852. [NRS.RD5.1756.461/76]

HUGGINS, JAMES P., born in Trinidad, graduated MB, CM, from Glasgow University in 1869. [RGG]

HUIE, JAMES, son of James Huie and his wife Margaret Haldane, died in Costa Rica on 16 March 1893. [East Preston Cemetery, Edinburgh]

HUME, HENRIETTA, daughter of .... Hume a land surveyor in Belize, married Alexander Williamson there on 6 August 1868. [S.7847]

HUMPHREY, WILLIAM, the younger, from Greenock in Renfrewshire, died in Demerara in 1813. [EA.5174.13]

HUNTER, ANDREW, a merchant in Leith, trading with New York and Jamaica from 1774 until 1777, a letter-book. [NRS.CS96.1986]

HUTCHEON, D., born in 1773, an army surgeon in Berbice, died on 7 March 1809. [SM.71.398]

HUTCHISON, JAMES, a merchant at the Bay of Honduras, died 178-. [NRS.CC8.130-132]

HUTTON, ALEXANDER, master of the Christian of Leith at Barbados in 1720. [NRS.HCAS.AC9.713]

HUTTON, DAVID, son of Alexander Hutton in Kinghorn, Fife, a merchant in Trinidad, died in Savanna Grande on 25 February 1852. [FJ]

HYNDMAN, WILLIAM, master of the Elizabeth of Greenock trading with St Kitts in 1744. [NRS.E504.15.1]

HYDE, DAVID, and Company, merchants in Greenock, trading with Honduras, Jamaica, and Demerara from 1814 until 1832. [NRS.CS96.870]

HYDE, JAMES, a merchant from Greenock in Renfrewshire, and a woodcutter in Honduras, deeds, 1814, 1820, and 1822. [NRS.RD5.63.5; RD5.177.225; CS17.1.42/63]

INGLIS, GEORGE, from Demerara, married Helen Alves, daughter of Dr John Inglis, a physician in Inverness, in Springfield on 24 July 1798. [SM..60.1798]; a planter in Demerara, was granted power of attorney by James Fraser of Belladrum in Inverness in 1795. [NRS.GD23.5.352]

INGLIS, GEORGE, from Inverness, a planter in Demerara before 1798. [RSSP.104]

INGLIS, JOHN, in Demerara, married Helen Alves, daughter of Dr John Alves a physician in Inverness on 24 July 1798. [SM.60.575]

INGRAM, ARCHIBALD, purchased land in St Kitts in 1765. [NRS.GD1.32.38.27]

INGRAM, GEORGE, a smith in Banff, in Trinidad by 1842.

INGRAM, ISAAC, in Antigua, and Guatamala, testament, 1874, Edinburgh. [NRS.SC70.1.168/600]

INNERARITY, ALEXANDER, a merchant in Glasgow and Demerara, versus Robert McKenzie in Demerara in 1836. [NRS.CS46.1836.6.148]

INNES, JOSEPH, of Pitmedden, a partner of an estate in Demerara, together with Henry Anderson and John Sutar of Grenada, from 1800 until his death in 1817. [NRS.CS96.1674/1817]

INNES, WILLIAM, from Demerara, married Elizabeth Donaldson, daughter of William Donaldson, in Elgin, Moray, in July 1801. [GC.1547]

INNES, WILLIAM, from Moray, a planter in Berbice in 1802. [RSSP.105]

IRVINE, C., took the Association Oath in Barbados on 14 May 1696. [TNA]

IRVINE, CHARLES WILLIAM, youngest son of John Irvine of the Chancery in Edinburgh, died in Tobago on 31 January 1810. [SM.72.317]

IRVINE, ROBERT, a merchant in Antigua, a sasine in Dumfries in 1729. [NRS.RS.Dumfries.10.480]

JACK, ROBERT, master of the Grange of Greenock from Greenock to Barbados in October 1779. [NRS.E504.5.31]

JACK, WILLIAM, a carpenter in Tobago, later a planter of Harmony Hall Estate, in North Naprina, Trinidad, a will dated on 31 August 1805. [NRS.GD44.34.54/3; his heirs were Josh Graham and Robert Mitchell in Tobago. [NRS.GD44.34.54/7]

JACKSON, Reverend JOHN, in Belize, British Honduras, father of a son born there on 25 December 1877, and another born there on 25 August 1883. [S.10793/S.12542]

JAFFRAY, DAVID, a manufacturer in Irvine, Ayrshire, trading with Quebec, Demerara, and Tobago from 1808 to 1809. [NRS.CS96.2047/2174]

JAMIESON, JAMES, a merchant, died in Demerara in 1818. [S.51.18]

JAMIESON, JAMES FERGUSON, a merchant in Trinidad and Demerara, testament, 1868. [NRS.SC70.1.140/505]

JEFFREY, ROBERT, of Irvine and of Demerara a Marriage Contract with Marion Hamilton dated 10 October 1880. [NRS.RD5.1782.446.297]

JOBSON, RACHEL SCOTT, eldest daughter of David Jobson a solicitor in Dundee, married John Gentle in Honduras on 16 November 1861. [S.2055]

JOHNSTON, ARCHIBALD, a surgeon, son of John Johnston, a writer [lawyer] in Bathgate, West Lothian, died in Berbice in December 1806. [SM.69.638]

JOHNSTOUN, ELIZABETH, born 1640, died on 18 July 1729. [St George's gravestone, Barbados]

JOHNSTON, MARGARET, eldest daughter of Dr Archibald Johnston in Berbice, died there on 26 January 1820. [BM.9.121]

JOHNSTON, ROBERT, master of the Mayflower of Glasgow from Port Glasgow to the West Indies on 5 October 1685. [NRS.E72.19.9]

JOHNSTON, RODERICK, a planter of Plantation Aurora, Essequibo, died on 20 March 1852, testament 1853, Edinburgh. [NRS].

JOHNSTONE, SARAH, daughter of Dr J. M. Johnstone late Health Officer of Demerara, married J. H. Dodd, government surveyor in Kingston, Jamaica on 24 July 1876.[S.10318]

JOHNSTON, WILLIAM, a surgeon, died in Demerara on 11 March 1829. [BM.26.268]

JOLLY, DAVID L., of Real de Monte, son of David L. Jolly, a banker in Perth, married Margaret Elizabeth Stewart MacGregor, youngest daughter of Robert MacGregor in Campbelltown, Argyll, in the British Consulate in Mexico on 2 April 1860. [DC.23504][W.21.2196][S1538]; his daughter was born in Tampico, Mexico, on 2 November 1873. [S.9449]

JOLLY, DAVID LEITCH, born 1833, was accidentally killed in Tampico, Mexico, on 10 December 1882. [S.12300]

JOLLY, ROBERT KEITH, fourth son of William Gairdner Jolly, died in Tampico, Mexico, on 30 May 1867. [S.7484]

JONES, MOSES, master of the Merchants Adventurers of Belfast arrived in Port Glasgow in September 1682 from Barbados. [NRS.E72.19.5]

KEITH, PATRICK, eldest son of Reverend Keith in Golspie, Sutherland, died in Berbice on 10 August 1805. [SM.68.78]

KEITH, THOMAS, in St Phillip's parish in Barbados in 1680. [TNA.CO1.44/47]

KELTIE, JOHN, only son of Robert Keltie in Demerara, died in London on 30 November 1819. [BM.3.60]

KENNEDY, JAMES, purchased land in Barbados in 1765. [NRS.GD1.32.38.27]

KENNEDY, JAMES LENNOX, born in Kirkcudbright, emigrated to New York in 1815, a merchant there and in Mazatlan, Mexico, US Consul there, died in Vera Cruz, Mexico, on 6 January 1887. [ANY.2.83]

KENNEDY, JOHN, purchased land in Nevis in 1765. [NRS.GD1.32.38.27]

KENNOWAY, WILLIAM THOMSON, died in San Jose, Costa Rica, on 1 February 1880. [FH]

KERR, ALEXANDER, a millwright in Edinburgh, settled in Jamaica by 1794. [NRS.AC7.67]

KERR, ROBERT, master of the Quebec of Greenock trading with Grenada in December 1782. [NRS.AC7.58]

KERR, ROBERT, in Grenada, a marriage contract with Elizabeth Ure, dated 24 February 1831. [NRS.RD5.1126.672/63]

KIDD, ALEXANDER, master of the Dolphin from Tobago to Dundee, arrived there on 20 May 1777. [NRS.E504.11.9]

KIDD, DAVID, master of the William and Ann arrived in Montrose in Angus on 17 January 1758 from Tobago via Madeira. [NRS.CE53.1.5]

KING, ..., master of the Gordon from Greenock to Antigua with a cargo of bale goods and herring in February 1758. [AJ]

KINLOCH, G. O., in Jamaica, a letter to James Wedderburn dated 6 February 1773, [NRS.GD1.8.36.3]

KINNISON, Reverend JOHN, in Demerara, a deed of factory dated 11 June 1860. [NRS.RD5.1120.234]

KIRK, JAMES, in Tobago, 1826-1849. [NRS.GD472]

KIRKE, ROBERT, born 1816, son of Robert Kirke and his wife Helen Balfour of Greenmount, Burntisland, Fife, of Waterloo, Nickerie, Surinam, died on 3 January 1894. [Cairneyhill gravestone in Fife]

KIRKBY, Colonel RICHARD, was Court Martialled in Port Royal, Jamaica, in October 1702. [NRS.GD45.24.28]

KIRKWOOD, Captain, master of the Pretty Jenny arrived in Greenock with a cargo of rum and sugar from Jamaica on 8 February 1758. [AJ]

KNIGHT, ADAM, from Portsoy in Banffshire, died in Demerara in 1808. [SM.70.477]

KNOX, JAMES, was born in Edinburgh during the 1690s, son of Reverend Henry Knox, became a minister on St Kitts. [F.2.172]

LAMBIE, ELIZABETH JANE, heir of William Lambie a planting attorney in Jamaica in 1882. [NRS.CS97.96.L2]

LAMONT, Captain, of the Resolution of Glasgow was captured by an American privateer in March 1779 when bound from St Kitts to Honduras. [AJ]

LANG, THOMAS, a merchant skipper in Greenock, trading with the West Indies between 1778 and 1788. [NRS.NRAS.1894]

LANG, WILLIAM, of Grenada, graduated MD, CM, from Glasgow University in 1863. [RGG]

LANKFORD, JOHN, from Barbados, died in Athlone, West Meath, Ireland, 1676, Prerogative Court of Canterbury. [TNA]

LAURIE, JAMES PITT, in Honduras, a letter to Colonel James Laurie concerning the political situation in Honduras on 10 June 1797. [NRS.GD461.31]

LAURIE, JAMES, eldest son of John Laurie in Glasgow, died on Curacao on 1 July 1809. [SM.70.799]

LAW, ALEXANDER, born 1782, son of James Law in Glasgow, died in Demerara in July 1802. [EA.4040.02

LAWRIE, Captain JAMES, master of the Sharp of Greenock trading with Grenada in 1776. [NRS.E504.15.26]

LAWRIE, Colonel JAMES, Superintendent of the Mosquito Coast [Nicaragua] papers from 1760 until 1799. [NRS.GD461.35.102]

LAWSON, ALEXANDER, master of the Dragon of London from Aberdeen on 13 November 1746 bound for Jamaica. [NRS.E505.1.2]

LAWSON, JOHN, born 1813, son of James Lawson [1769-1827], and his wife Elizabeth Smart, died on passage from Dominica on 24 February 1843. [Constitution Road gravestone, Dundee]

LAWSON, PETER, son of James Lawson [1769-1827] and his wife Elizabeth Smart, was drowned off Dominica on 17 February 1828. [Constitution Road gravestone, Dundee]

LEITH, Lieutenant General Sir JAMES, Governor of the Windward Islands and the Leeward Islands, papers in 1815. [NRS.GD225.984]

LESLIE, GEORGE, late in Jamaica, later in Old Aberdeen, testament, 24 May 1796, Comm. Aberdeen. [NRS]

LESLIE, Colonel John, was buried on 8 March 1711 in Barbados. [St John's burial register]

LESLIE, Reverend purchased land in St Kitts in 1765. [NRS.GD1.32.38.27]

LESLIE, WILLIAM, first Rector of St John's, Barbados, 1653 grandson of John Leslie, eighth Baron of Balquhain. [St John' MI, Barbados]

LESLIE, WILLIAM, manager of Sans Souci Estate, in St Vincent, son of James Leslie farmer at Boggs of Main, near Elgin, Moray, died of cholera on Sans Souci Estate on 26 September 1854. [IA]

LEWIS, Captain GEORGE C. D., letters from Barbados and Trinidad in 1836. [NRS.GD15.2425]

LEWIS, JOSEPH, in Jamaica, a Deed of Factory to Christopher Douglas a Writer to the Signet, dated 4 April 1861. [NRS.RD5.1127.195/65]

LEWIS, WILLIAM, and MATTHEW LEWIS, planters in Jamaica in 1778. [NRS.HCAS.AC7.56]

LINDON, WILLIAM, purchased land in Grenada in 1765. [NRS.GD1.32.38.27]

LOABY, MORGAN, purchased land in St Eustatius in 1765. [NRS.GD1.32.38.27]

LIZARS, WILLIAM, in Georgetown, British Guina, son and heir of William Lizars a shoemaker in Leith, Midlothian, in 1833. [NRS.S/H]

LOABY, MORGAN, purchased land in St Eustatius in 1765. [NRS.GD1.32.38.27]

LOCH, Captain, paymaster aboard HMS Alarm off the Mosquito Coast in June 1847, also the ship's log. [NRS.GD268.997]

LOTHIAN, JOHN, born 1842, son of Robert Lothian in Kingsbarns, Fife, died on Dukenfield Estate, St Thomas in the East, Jamaica, on 27 July 1883. [EFR]

LOW, WILLIAM, a merchant, died in Berbice on 8 June 1802. [EA.4054.02][GKA.88]

LOWDOUN, GEORGE, a cloth merchant in Glasgow, trading with Jamaica, Martinique, New York and San Domingo between 1819 and 1821. [NRS.CS16.768]

LYLE, JOHN, formerly a merchant in Nevis, last in Gourock, 18.. [NRS.CS271.586]

LYON, GEORGE, master of the Walter of Wairwater bound from the West Indies to the River Clyde in 1685. [NRS.HCAS.AC7.7]

LYON, JAMES, master of the Lilly of Glasgow from Greenock to St Kitts in January 1770. [NRS.E504.15.18]

LYON, JAMES, and Company, merchants in Kingston, Jamaica, in 1788. [NRS.HCASAC7.62]

MCADAM, JEAN, of Craigengillan, married Lieutenant Colonel Frederick Cathcart in Berbice on 18 October 1827. [EEC.18113]

MACALISTER, ALEXANDER, born in Demerara, graduated MD from Glasgow University in 1851. [RGG]

MACALISTER, RANALD, third son of Dr MacAlister of Strathaird in Skye, Inverness-shire, died in Demerara on 31 March 1820. [BM.7.583]

MACALISTER, THOMAS, in St Lucy's, Barbados, in 1679. [TNA.CO1.44/47]

MCANDIE, JAMES, in British Guiana around 1855. [NRS.242/70/6/183, Tain]

MCARTHUR, CHARLES, father of a daughter born in Georgetown, Demerara, on 21 September 1863. [S.2599]

MCARTHUR, DONALD, son of John McArthur of Ardgavannan in Argyll, died on his way home from Demerara aboard the schooner Diana in July 1800. [NRS.CC2.8.105]

MACARTNEY, ALEXANDER, second son of Reverend William MacCartney in Old Kilpatrick, Dunbartonshire, died in Arequibo, Puerto Rico on 3 December 1833. [SG.3.241]

MACARTNEY, JAMES, a merchant in Mexico, died in Edinburgh on 22 August 1839, testament, 1839. [NRS.SC70.1.58/426]

MCAULAY, JAMES, lately from Honduras, died in Exeter, England, during 1795. [GM.65.174]

MCAULAY, Captain of the Lord Belhaven from Grenock t S Domingo on 2 May 1819. [EEC.16836]

MCBEAN, ANN MARY, in Christianstad, Danish West Indies, probate 31 January 1826. [RAK]

MCBEAN, WILLIAM, from Tomatin, Inverness-shire, a merchant and partner of Sandbach, Tinne and Company in Demerara from 1803 until around 1808. [RSSP.116]

MCBEATH, Dr WILLIAM, born 25 February 1764 in Inverness, a physician in Demerara, died on 11 October 1797. [Chapel Yard gravestone, Inverness]

MCCALMONT, HUGH, born 1801, died in Demerara during 1838. [St Andrew's Scots Church gravestone, Demerara]

MCCARTY, MARIA, daughter of James McCarty in Martinique, married George Young a merchant in Edinburgh on 14 June 1800. [EMR]

MCCASKILL, KENNETH, a surgeon, died on the Hague Plantation in Essequibo, on 11 September 1818. [EA.5749.79]CS96.169]

MACCASKEY, ALLEN, in St Joseph's, Barbados, in 1680. [TNA.CO1.44/47]

MCCAUL, JOHN, a merchant in Glasgow, trading with St Croix in the Danish West Indies, also with Trinidad, in 1831 to 1832. [NRS.]

MCCLELLAN, Reverend ALEXANDER, son of George McClellan [1783-1835] and his wife Elizabeth Gordon, in Borgue, Kirkcudbrightshire, minister of St James in Demerara from1862, died on17 May 1838. [TMG.1/280; S/372]

MCCLELLAND, JOHN, died in San Salvador during August 1832, testament 1835 in Edinburgh. [NRS]

MCCLURE, JAMES, born in Ayr on 17 October 1763, son of David McClure and his wife Ann Kennedy, a geologist who died at San Angel in Mexico 23 March 1843.
[WA]

MCCOMBIE, ALEXANDER, born 1786 in Aberdeen, emigrated in 1806. Died on St Lucia on 22 April 1865. [AJ]

MCCOOK, FRANCIS, born 1790 in Old Meldrum, Aberdeenshire, died in Kingston, Jamaica, on 17 November 1850. [AJ]

MCCULLOCH, GEORGE, Major of the Militia in St Catherine's, Jamaica, in 1776. [IRO][TNA.WO].

MCCULLOCH, JOHN, in the sugar estate, Unidad, Partido de Calabazar, Sagua la Grande, Cuba, testament, 1888. [NRS.SC70.1.264/338]

MCCUNE, THOMAS, son of Samuel McCune in Wigtownshire, was educated at Glasgow University, a minister in British Guiana in 1845. [F.7.675]

MCCURLY, ALEXANDER, master of the Castle Semple was bound via Cork for St Kitts, later changed to Antigua, by 1784. [NRS.HCAS.AC7.61]

MCDONALD, ALEXANDER, was educated at Aberdeen University, minister of St Mary's, British Guiana from 1838 until 1841. [F.7.679]

MACDONALD, ALLAN, from Scotland, a planter in Berbice in 1802. [RSSP.106]; late in Berbice, Demerara, died 3 May 1849. [Duddingston gravestone, Midlothian]

MCDONALD, A., in Demerara, around 1830. [NRS.GD1.641.49]

MCDONALD, DONALD, brother of Clanranald, a student in Leiden, Utrecht, and Amsterdam, later a Revenue Officer in Demerara and Berbice, letters from 1817 until 1834. [NRS.GD201.4.96]; died in Berbice in February 1838. [AJ.4717]

MCDONALD, FRANCIS, born in Caithness, died in Berbice in March 1830. [NS]

MCDONALD, GORDON, of Plantation Moy, Corome, Surinam, died in Burntisland, Fife, on 28 June 1859. [Burntisland gravestone]

MCDONALD, JOHN, in Berbice, eldest son of Donald McDonald sometime in Jamaica, a deed dated 5 October 1809. [NRS.RD2.307.259]

MCDONALD, JOHN, born 1820, died in Kingston, Jamaica, on 13 January 1898. [S.17041]

MACDONALD, JOSEPH, in Demerara, a letter dated 5 April 1800. [NRS.GD47.684]

MCDONALD, WILLIAM, a planter in Jamaica, husband of Ann Campbell, a sasine in Edinburgh in 1768. [NRS.RS27.179.206-211]

MCDONALD, Mrs, widow of John McDonald of Plantation Kintyre in Berbice, married Alexander McDuff, a Lieutenant of the 100th Regiment of Foot, on 18 November 1824. [S.508.829]; and children in Berbice, an agreement with Mrs MacDuff, 2 June 1832. [NRS.RD468.517, 160]

MCDOUGALL, JAMES, born 1848, a joiner third son of James McDougall in Eskdalerig, St Mungo, died in Georgetown, Demerara, on 8 October 1881. [Annandale Observer]

MCDOWELL, Dr ANDREW, in Barbados, a letter re slaves – their numbers, costs, illnesses causing their deaths, in August 1731. [NRS.CS228.A.3.19/43]

MCEACHRAN, ARCHIBALD, born in 1823, died in Belize, Honduras, on 6 February 1855. [IA]

MCEWAN, ALEXANDER LOW, in Essequibo, British Guiana, died on 26 February 1863. [NRS.S/H.29.9.1885]

MCEWAN, JOHN, son of William McEwan [1768-1832], died in Mexico in 1832. [Logerait gravestone, Perthshire]

MACFARLANE, ANDREW, in Jamaica, a letter to his sister, dated 9 November 1782. [SRA.T-MJ 369]

MACFARLANE, Reverend ANDREW, assistant to Reverend Dr Struthers, died in Georgetown, Demerara, on 5 September 1839. [AJ.4974][SG.8.815]

MACFARLANE, DUNCAN, Lieutenant of the Horse Militia in Jamaica in 1776. [IRO][TNA.WO]

MCFARLANE, HELEN, eldest daughter of P.McFarlane in Faslane, Dunbartonshire, married Robert Smith MD, in Berbice on 28 June 1839. [SG.8.809]

MCFARLANE, Captain, master of the Friends of Glasgow when bound home from the Leeward Islands was captured by an American privateer, but was later liberated by a Liverpool privateer and taken to Cork in October 1778. [AJ]

MACFENNY, OWEN, was buried in St Joseph's, Barbados, on 7 August 1678. [TNA.CO1.44/47]

MACFARLANE, JAMES, in Demerara, a deed dated 1845. [NRS.RD5.758.681]

MCFARLAN, ROBERT, born 30 December 1787 in Glasgow, a merchant in Jamaica, late of Carthagena, Columbia, died in Lauriston, Glasgow, on 8 December 1827. [Ramshorn gravestone]

MCFARQUHAR, JOHN, in Bellevue, late of Demerara, died in Greenock on 26 September 1839. [SG.8.816]

MCGHONACHIE, JOHN, son of George McGhonachie, schoolmaster of Logie-Pert in Angus [died 1844] and his wife Helen Rennie [died 1846], died in Honduras on 13 September 1832. [Pert gravestone, Angus]

MCGILL, A. T., bandmaster of the 1st Battalion of the Royal Scots Regiment, married Hannah, daughter of William Quayle Douglas from the Isle of Man, in Barbados on 1 October 1884. [S.12888]

MACGILL, JOHN WHYTE, born in Musselburgh, Midlothian, 21 August 1867, son of Henry Moncrieff MacGill, graduated MA from Edinburgh University in 1889, a minister in British Guiana from 1897 until 1924. [F.6.225]

MCGOUN, ARCHIBALD, in Mexico, nephew and heir of Robert McGoun, a merchant in Greenock, Renfrewshire, who died on 28 February 1846. [NRS.S/H]

MCGOUN, ARCHIBALD, born 1809 son of Duncan McGoun in Glasgow, died in Zatetacas, Mexico, on 29 October 1878. [EC.29400]

MCGOUN, JOHN STUART, MD, died in Acapulco, Mexico, in 1851. [NRS.S/H.1871] [S.17.1,1852]

MCGOUN, LAUCHLAN CAMPBELL, born 1817, son of Duncan McGoun a merchant in Glasgow, matriculated at Glasgow University in 1831, to New York by 1850, settled ar Guanaxuhato, Mexico, by 1870; he married Ellen Bell in Edinburgh on 30 January 1868, she died at Guanaxuata on 4 January 1869. [NRS.SH.1870/1871][MAGU.12869] [ANY.2.229]

MCGOWAN, JAMES, born 1796, son of William McGowan, [1756-1831], and his wife Grizel Callendar, [1762-1813], a merchant in Castries, St Lucia, died on 25 February 1834. [Crossmichael gravestone, Kirkcudbrightshire]

MCGREGOR, DUNCAN, born 1811, died on La Bonne Intention Estate in Demerara in July 1844. [Faslane gravestone, Jamaica Dunbartonshire]

MCGREGOR, GRACE ROSS, eldest daughter of Ranald McGregor in Banff, died on 27 April 1859 at Pleasant Hill House in Jamaica. [Pleasant Hill gravestone, Jamaica]

MCGREGOR, JAMES, a merchant, only son of ....MacGregor in St Andrews Square in Edinburgh, died in Georgetown, Demerara, on 12 June 1825. [BM.18,655]

MACGREGOR, JAMES SCOTT, born 1847, son of MacGregor of the Royal Hotel in Dundee, also nephew of Robert Scott of the Spread Eagle Hotel in Jedburgh, Roxburghshire, died in Demerara on 2 July 1874. [S.9678]

MCGREGOR, JOHN W., in Rora, St Anne's, , a letter to Sir James Grant dated 10 September 1791. [NRS.GD248.362.5]

MACGREGOR, JOHN MALCOLM, in Mandeville, Jamaica, was served heir to his grand-mother Margaret Anderson, widow of John MacGregor in Dufftown, Banffshire, who died on 12 December 1898. [NRS.S/H]

MCGRIGOR, DAVID, born in 1799, son of Alexander McGrigor and his wife Ann Mackay, a house carpenter at La Belle Alliance in Demerara, died on 15 September 1839. [Croik gravestone in Strath Carron]

MCGUFFIE, JAMES MUIR, Her Majesty's Consul in Gonaives, Haiti, died in New York on 30 August 1849. [GM.ns.32.559]

MCGUFFIE, JOHN, minister of St Saviour's in British Guiana from 1862 until 1878. [F.7.680]

MCGUSTY, JOHN MURRAY, married Madelaine Gordon, fourth daughter of William Gordon of Aberdour in Fife, in Georgetown, Demerara, on 20 June 1825. [S.587.543]

MCHARDY, GEORGE, born in 1803, son of Charles McHardy [1745-1811] a schoolmaster, and his wife Henrietta Murray, [1767-1819, died in Jamaica on 9 March 1821. [Fetteresso gravestone, Kincardineshire]

MCILWRAITH, ROBERT, born 1756, a merchant in Greenock, died in Tobago. [Inverkip Street gravestone, Greenock, Renfrewshire].

MCINROY, JAMES, born 1759, from Moulin in Perthshire, a planter and merchant in Demerara, a partner by 1792 in Sandbach, Tinne and Company, died in 1825. [RSSP.116]

MCINROY, JAMES, in Demerara, married Elizabeth Moore of St Eustatia, in Broomloan on 25 December 1797. [EEC.420]

MCINROY, ..., a planter at Phoenix Park, Demerara, before 1833. [NRS.GD132.796]

MCINTOSH, CATHERINE, daughter of Alexander McIntosh in Paramaribo, Surinam, married Johan Leng Hutchler in Nymegen in the Netherlands on 1 November 1876 . [S.10,390]

MACINTOSH, CHARLES, born 1782, eldest son of Alexander MacIntosh and his wife Janet McLean, drowned in the River Essequibo on 21 April 1814. [Greyfriars gravestone, Inverness]

MCINTOSH, DONALD, was educated at King's College in Aberdeen, minister of St Mark's in British Guiana from 1829 until 1837. [F.7.679]

MACKINTOSH, EWAN CLARK, born 1811, died in Tacbaya, Mexico, in 1861. [S.1885]

MCINTOSH, GEORGE, a Lieutenant of the 60th [Royal American] Regiment in Jamaica in 1776. [IRO][TNA.WO]

MCINTOSH, HENRY, a reference in 1675, planter on Sukika Creek, Commewijne, Surinam, in 1680s. [SPAWI.291.402]; a planter in Surinam, married Elizabeth Le Hunt from Port Royal, Jamaica.in 1688, died in

Surinam in 1690; [CSP.1675.01] [Abstracts of New York Wills, liber 1-2, pp184-186][SPAWI.1675.401]

MACKINTOSH, HENRY ALEXANDER, born 1808, died in Mineral dela Luz, Mexico, on 3 September 1860. [DC.23550]

MCINTOSH, JOHN, born 1864, from Braenalion, Glencairn, Ballater, in Aberdeenshire, died in San Jose de Guatamala in Mexico on 6 March 1900. [AJ.17.4.1900]; testament, 1900, Edinburgh. [NRS]

MACKINTOSH, LOUIS ALEXANDER, Her Majesty's Consul, married Isabella Bathgate Marr, third daughter of James Marr of Adeston MD, MRCPE, in Paramaribo, Dutch Guiana, on 4 January 1871. [S.8590]; father of a son born in Surinam on 1 June 1872. [S.9025]

MACKINTOSH, MARION SUSAN ANNE READE, only daughter of Thomas Mackintosh in Guadaloupe y Calvo in Mexico, married William Randolph Simpson, RA, in Southsea, England, on 13 August 1853. [GM.ns40.522]

MACKINTOSH, RONALD MARR, an infant son of Louis A. Mackintosh, died in Paramaribo, Dutch Guiana on 8 October 1874. [S.9776]

MACKINTOSH, THOMAS, in Guadaloupe y Calvo, Mexico, in 1853. [GM.ns.40.5220]

MCINTOSH, WILLIAM, son of Alexander McIntosh [1769-1802], a merchant in Inverness, settled in Surinam before 1843. [Kilmallie gravestone, Argyll]

MACKINTOSH, WILLIAM LYSTER HAY, born 1824, died in Guanasevi, Mexico, on 21 May 1856. [GM.ns.2/1.390]

MCINTYRE, DANIEL, born 8 November 1778, in Glenorchy, Argyll, son of Joseph McIntyre and his wife Christian McVean, was educated at St Andrews University from 1791 to 1793, possibly died in Jamaica in July 1797. [SAU]

MCINTYRE, DONALD, a surgeon of the 43rd Regiment of Foot in America 1781, Inspector General of Hospitals in the Leeward Islands in 1796, graduated MD in 1803, died on 28 November 1815. [SAU]

MCINTYRE, JOHN, formerly a merchant in Liverpool, died in Demerara on 4 July 1824. [S.487.666]

MCINTYRE, PATRICK, died in Demerara on 12 August 1821.
[BM.10.489]

MACKAY, AENEAS, son of James Mackay in Ross-shire, died in Havanna, Cuba, in May 1817. [GM.61.186]

MACKAY, DANIEL, from St Croix, married Mrs John Muir, a widow in Demerara, in Edinburgh on 17 February 1825. [GM.ns.95.273]

MACKAY, DONALD, in Demerara in 1802. [NRS.GD23.6.391]

MCKAY, GRISSEL, born 1750, died in Barbados on 19 September 1787. [St Lucy's gravestone]

MCKECHNIE, Dr JOHN, a medical student in Edinburgh, later a physician in Demerara around 1809. [NRS.CS97.102.49; CS17.1.20.511]

MCKELLAR, DUNCAN, a merchant in Greenock, trading with Antigua in 1796. [NRS.E504.15.73]

MACKENHASS, ..., [MacInnes or MacAoghais?], in Surinam, a petitioner in the 1670s. [TNA.CO1.26.81]

MACKENNY, DANIEL, in St Lucy's, Barbados, in 1679. [TNA.CO1.44/47]

MACKENNY, GILBERT, in St Lucy's, Barbados, in 1679. [TNA.CO1.44/47]

MACKENNY, THOMAS, the younger, was buried in St Joseph's, Barbados, on 28 January 1678. [TNA.CO1.44/47]

MCKENZIE, ALEXANDER, born 1783, second son of George McKenzie of Pitlundy, died in Demerara in 1802. [SM.44.448]

MCKENZIE, Dr ALEXANDER, LLD, born 1770, died in Demerara on 15 September 1828. [SM.25268] [St Andrews Scots Church gravestone, Demerara]

MCKENZIE, CHARLES, died in Demerara on 13 May 1839. [SG.8.783]

MACKENZIE, DEVONIA, wife of George Knox, die in Georgetown, Demerara, on 26 January 1868. [S.7672]

MCKENZIE, GEORGE, son of John McKenzie in Edinburgh, a merchant in Bridgetown, Barbados, probate 28 August 1711, Barbados.

MACKENZIE, HECTOR, from Clyne in Sutherland, a planter in Berbice in 1802. [RSSP.105]

MCKENZIE, HUGH, born 1821, son of Reverend David McKenzie, died in Demerara during 1844. [Farr gravestone, Sutherland]

MCKENZIE, JANE, late in Demerara, died in Edinburgh on 3 September 1825, testament, 1836. [NRS]

MCKENZIE, JOHN, third son of Charles McKenzie, a writer [lawyer] in Edinburgh, died in Demerara in 1802. [GkAd.54]

MCKENZIE, Dr SIMON, in Jamaica, son of Dr John McKenzie in Fortrose, Easter Ross, died in Fortrose, Honduras, on 2 August 1797. [SM.49.621]

MCKENZIE, WILLIAM, born 1847, son of William McKenzie and his wife Jane Thompson in Carron, Easter Ross, died in Surinam on 10 December 1893. [Aberlour gravestone, Banffshire]

MCKINNON, DANIEL, took the Association Oath in Antigua in 1696. [TNA]

MCKNIGHT, WILLIAM, supercargo aboard the snow John and David of Port Glasgow bound for Barbados in 1727. [NRS.HCAS.AC10.138]

MCKINLAY, ROBERT, a merchant in Greenock, trading with Antigua in 1796. [NRS.E504.15.73]

MCKINNON, DANIEL, took the Association Oath in Antigua in 1696. [TNA]; born 1658, a physician who settled in Antigua, husband of Elizabeth Thomas, probate 20 March 1720 in Antigua.

MCKNIGHT, WILLIAM, supercargo aboard the snow John and David of Port Glasgow bound for Barbados in 1727. [NRS.HCAS.AC10.138]

MACKRAY, PATRICK, a merchant in Demerara, son of Robert MacKray in Aberdeen, a deed dated 27 June 1824. [NRS.RD5.275.8]

MACLACHLAN, BLANCHE, eldest daughter of R. S. MacLachlan, married William F. Bliss, in Brighton, St Ann's, Jamaica, on 29 July 1884. [S.12833]

MCLAREN, ROBERT, a merchant and planter in Demerara, subscribed to his last will and testament in Georgetown, Demerara on 20 June 1814, [NRS.RD5.182.697]; he died on his voyage home from Demerara on 6 June 1820. [BM.7.584]

MCLARTY, ARCHIBALD, a shipmaster in Greenock, master of the Britannia, trading with Jamaica in April 1769. [NRS.AC7.53]

MACLARTY, Dr COLIN, in Jamaica, a letter to his father, dated 23 July 1792. [NLS. John Cunningham letters, Acc.7285]

MCLAUGHLIN, HUGH, sr., a merchant from Leith, emigrated with his family aboard the snow Adventure, master James Hamilton who settled in Kingston, Jamaica, by 1755. [NRS.HCAS.C7.47.598]

MCLAURIN, EWAN, late Captain of the Breadalbane Fencibles [a militia unit], son of Lieutenant Colonel McLaurin of the South Carolina Loyalists, died in Demerara on 5 May 1810. [EA]

MCLAURIN, Mrs, widow of Ewan McLaurin in Charleston, America and sister of Bain Whyte, a Writer to the Signet in Edinburgh, died in Demerara on 2 December 1822. [SM.91.519]

MCLEAN, DANIEL, and his spouse, on St Vincent, a deed of factory and commission to Ann Allardyce, dated 6 January 1863. [NRS.RD118.701]

MCLEAN, JOHN, a merchant in Kingston, Jamaica, dead by 1769, owner of the Edinburgh which was shipwrecked when bound for Jamaica. [NRS.HCAS.AC7.53]

MCLEAN, SAMUEL, master of the Three Brothers from St Thomas in the Dutch West Indies, bound for Amsterdam in 1777. [GAA.NA.15601/319]

MCLEAN, THOMAS, in St Joseph's, Barbados, father of Thomas who was baptised there 1679. [TNA.CO1.44/47]

MCLEOD, DANIEL, in St Lucy's, Barbados, in 1679. [TNA.CO1.44/47]

MCLEOD, DANIEL, born 1709, died in Barbados on 18 June 1759. [St Joseph's gravestone]

MCLEOD, DONALD, son of Andrew McLeod in Sutherland, died in Berbice in 1849. [IA]

MCLEOD, GEORGE, in the Bahamas in 1820s, his father William McLeod in Dysart, Fife, wrote to the Earl of Roslyn seeking patronage for his son. [NRS.GD164.1767]

MCLEOD, GEORGE, son of John McLeod of Milne, Cruden and Company in Aberdeen, chief government clerk in Castries, died in St Lucia on 14 February 1864. [AJ]

MCLEOD, HUGH, a merchant in Kingston, Jamaica, died in 1819, partner of John Miller and John Ure in Glasgow, also Joseph Downie in Aux Cayes, Haiti, 1815-1819. [NRS.CS96.2311]

MCLEOD, JOHN, of Colbecks, St Dorothy's, Jamaica, married Margaret McLeod, daughter of Roderick McLeod a Writer to the Signet, in Edinburgh on 29 November 1773. [EMR]

MCLEOD, JOHN, son of Andrew McLeod in Sutherland, died in Demerara in summer 1849. [IA]

MCLETCHIE, WILLIAM, a merchant in Tobago, a bond dated 1800. [NRS.CS271.373]

MCLINTOCK, Captain, master of the Port Glasgow from Glasgow with a cargo of herring bound for Antigua on 1 December 1753. [AJ]

MCNAB, CHARLES, from Jamaica, married Janet Buchanan, daughter of Dougal Buchanan of Craigievorn in Stirlingshire, in Edinburgh on 1 October 1792. [EMR]

MCNAIR, JAMES, a merchant and sugar refiner in Greenock, trading with Demerara from 1820 until 1821. [NRS.CS96.4260]

MACNAUGHT, WILLIAM, in St Lucy's, Barbados, in 1679. [TNA.CO1.44/47]

MACNEAL, HECTOR, was born on 22 October 1746 in Rosebank, Roslin, Midlothian, later in St Kitts, Guadaloupe, St George's in Grenada, and Kingston, Jamaica. [NRS.NRAS.0052] 104

MCNEILL, HECTOR, a Lieutenant of the 50th [Queen's Own] Regiment, stationed in Jamaica around 1776. [TNA.WO][IRO]

MCNEIL, NEIL, a partner of McNeil, Saddler and Company, merchants in St Kitts from 1758 until 1781, absconded to St Croix in the Danish West Indies around 1780. [NRS.C96.4370]

MCPHERSON, ALEXANDER, in St Phillip's parish in Barbados in 1680. [TNA.CO1.44/47]

MCNEILL, WILLIAM, of Hayfield, a merchant in Glasgow, with plantations in Essequibo and in Trinidad, trading with Demerara, Tobago, Trinidad, Jamaica, and Barbados, from 1806 to 1808. [NRS.CS96.966/967]

MCNEILL, STEWART, and Company, owners of the Aurra Plantation and the Makeshift Plantation in Essquibo, records from 1806 until 1808, also a letterbook from 1810 until 1817. [NRS.C96.966-967]

MCNISH, D., in Bermuda, a letter to Captain Archibald McDonald of the 2nd West India Regiment in Jamaica, dated 28 February 1807. [NRS.GD47.754]

MACPETRIE, JAMES, son of James MacPetrie in Aberdeen was educated at King's College in Aberdeen, later a surgeon in Tobago. [KCA]

MCPHERSON, EWEN, from Demerara, married Catherine Campbell McGregor, eldest daughter of Alexander McGregor of St Andrews Square, Edinburgh, in Edinburgh in 1817. [S.17.17]

MCPHERSON, WILLIAM, son of Allan McPherson and his wife Elizabeth in Blairgowrie, Perthshire, a planter in Berbice from 1806. [NRS.NRAS.bundle 8.10]

MACRAE, ALEXANDER, from Inverinate in Wester Ross, a planter in Demerara, in 1798. [RSSP.104]

MACRAE, ALEXANDER, a Member of the Court of Policy in Demerara, also Chief of his name in the Highlands of Scotland, died in Demerara in June 1812. [SM.74.727]

MCRAE, DONALD, in Demerara, a letter to Simon Fraser, a shoemaker in Church Street, Inverness, dated 24 July 1801. [HCA.D122/2/3]

MACREDIE, ..., daughter of W. M. MacRedie, was born in Nickerie, Surinam, on 9 October 1881. [S.11,961]

MACREDIE, ALICE, wife of William MacRedie, died in Nickerie, Surinam, on 19 August 1884. [ASS.12849]

MCROB, DUNCAN, master of the Friendship from the Clyde bound for Antigua on 18 November 1782, the ship was severely storm damaged and was captured by an American privateer Commander on 24 January 1783, however on 26 January 1783 HMS Enterprize appeared and the ship was released and taken to Island Harbour in Antigua. [NRS.HCAS.AC7.61]

MACSWINE, OWEN, in St Lucy's, Barbados, in 1679. [TNA.CO1.44/47]

MACVICAR, C. R. DAVIDSON, of Cyrilton and Dearg, died in Vera Cruz, Mexico, on 2 October 1883. [S.12556]

MALLOCH, JOHN, master of the Dolphin from Leith with passengers bound for Darien on the Isthmus of Panama on 14 July 1698. [NRS.GD406, Bc23/3.b161, 25/23]shment

MANDERS, ROBERT, from Dunbarton, bound from the Netherlands for the West Indies, testament, 16 December 1623. [GAR.ONA.104/125/191]

MANSON, WILLIAM, son of James Manson, a merchant in Rotterdam, and his wife Margaret Gray, grandson of Alexander Manson, a merchant in Thurso, Caithness, and his wife Elizabeth Munro, died in 1801 on Curacao, Dutch West Indies. [CFH.323]

MANTACH, Reverend ROBERT, born 1798 in Elgin, Moray, died on Boaz Island, Chaplain to the Convict Establishment, in Bermuda on 18 January 1854. [IA]

MANUEL, JOHN, emigrated from Cupar in Fife to the West Indies on I April 1867. [FH]

MARTIN, GEORGE, in Tortula in 1821. [NRS.CS17.1.40/8]

MARTIN, HENRY, master of the Mayflower of New York arrived in Glasgow in October 1683 from Barbados. [NRS.E72.19.8]

MARTIN, JAMES, born in Aberdeenshire, a planter in Grenada, died upon the Ferrier bound to Tobago in 1839. [AJ]

MARTIN, JOHN, master of the Mayflower of Liverpool from Port Glasgow bound for the West Indies on 25 Januay 1682. [NRS.E72.19.6]

MARTIN, THOMAS, a merchant, died in Demerara on 10 December 1820. [BM.8.708]

MASSON, JAMES, born 1849, son of Alexander Masson in Harthills, Kintore, died in Berbice, British Guina, on 24 January 1875. [AJ]

MATHESON, ALEXANDER GORDON, youngest son of Colin Matheson of Bennetsfield, died in Berbice on 13 October 1820. [BM.8.482]

MATHIE, HUGH, a merchant in Glasgow, trading with Nassau, New Providence, Quebec, Baltimore, Virginia, Montreal, the West Indies, and Martinique around 1803. [NRS.CS96.3231]

MATTHEW, SAMUEL, born 1837, eldest sn of James Matthew of the High Court of Justiciary in Edinburgh, died in Port of Spain, Trinidad, on 30 November 1859. [CM.21615]

MAULL, CATHERINE, heir to her father Reverend James Maull in Antigua, in 1697. [NRS.S/H]

MAULE, JOHN, son of Charles Maule in Leith, a merchant in Demerara, died there on 17 October 1798. [AJ.2664] [GC.1159]

MAXTON, JAMES, of the 57th Regiment stationed at Halifax, Nova Scotia, and in the West Indies, letters from 1788 until 1800. [NRS.GD155.866]

MAXTON, PETER, was killed by pirates in San Domingo before 1800. [NRS.CS22.780.26]

MAXTON, THOMAS, an officer of the Royal Navy, letters from America, Bermuda, and Halifax, Nova Scotia, from 1788 until 1796. [NRS.GD155.865]

MAXWELL, JAMES, a surgeon in Jamaica, heir to his father James Maxwell a manufacturer in Dundee, in 1838. [NRS.S/H]

MAXWELL, JAMES, of the 1st West India Regiment, an inventory dated 1874. [NRS.SC70.170.17]

MAXWELL, THOMAS, took the Association Oath in Barbados on 14 May 1695. [TNA]

MEIKLE, JOHN, in Demerara, died in 1807. [NRS.RH4.189]

MEINE, PATRICK, took the Association Oath in Barbados on 14 May 1696. [TNA]

MELVILLE, ALEXANDER, in St Vincent, graduated MD from Edinburgh University in 1811. [EMG]

MELVILLE, D., a merchant in Berbice, married Sarah, daughter of John Polson, in Old Aberdeen, in 1828. [S.846.114]

MELVILLE, JAMES, eldest son of John Melville in Back Lebanon, Cupar, Fife, died in San Jose, Costa Rica, on 11 October 1861. [H]

MELVILL, ROBERT, the Governor General of Grenada, a sasine in Edinburgh in 1765. [NRS.RS27.167.347]

MENZIES, JOHN, a merchant from Glasgow, died in St Eustatia, Dutch West Indies, on 18 February 1781. [SM.43.223]

MENZIES, JOHN, of Plantation Zeelugt in Demerara, son of Neil Menzies in Anstruther in Fife, married Adrina, daughter of Donald Cameron of Plantation Zeelugt on 30 September 1865. [EFR]

MERCHANT, WILLIAM COPLAND, born 1821, son of William Merchant [1771-1822]and his wife Elizabeth Wilson [died 1854], an engineer who died in Tobago on 5 September 1852. [St Nicholas gravestone, Aberdeen]

MIDDLETON, GEORGE, born 1810, son of Reverend George Middleton in Midmar, Aberdeenshire, died of yellow fever in Jamaica on 28 November 1852. [AJ]

MILL, JAMES, in St Michael's, Barbados, son of Robert Mill of Belfray, father of David, a sasine in Edinburgh dated 1761. [NRS.RS27.151.437]

MILLER, ARCHIBALD, emigrated from Scotland to the West Indies in 1769, a mason there until 1781. [TNA.AO100.348]

MILLER, GEORGE, in Long Island in the Bahamas in 1795. [NRS.CS17.1.14/99]

MILLER, JAMES, master of the Hope from Leith with passengers bound for Darien in Panama in 1698.

MILLER, JAMES, late merchant in New Providence in the Bahamas, now in Edinburgh, versus Elisabeth Fowler, spouse of Dr Mitchell in Virginia, 1815. [NRS.GD63.478]

MILLER, ROBERT, master of the Nancy of Leith from St Kitts to London in 1776. [NRS.HCA.AC7.58.2]

MILLIKEN, HUGH, a merchant in Port Glasgow, trading with Antigua, Grenada, Jamaica, St Kitts, St Vincent, and Quebec from 1800 until 1808. [NRS.CS96.4361]

MILNE, ALEXANDER, born 1781, Lieutenant Colonel of the 19th Regiment, died in Demerara on 5 November 1827. [Demerara gravestone]

MILNE, ALEXANDER, born 1804 in Skene, Aberdeenshire, a mason on the Content Estate, Hanover, Jamaica, died there on 3 October 1837. [AJ]

MILNE, JOHN, born 1813, youngest son of Alexander Milne og the Mains of Skene, died on Hopewell Estate, Hanover, Jamaica, on 1 September 1841. [AJ]

MILNE, ROBERT, born on 22 April 1775, son of Reverend James Milne and his wife Jean, a merchant in St Domingo, died on 9 September 1814. [F.6.330]

MILNE, ROBERT, son of Thomas Milne in Auchlie in Aberdeenshire, emigrated to the Netherlands in 1696, from there to Curacao in the Dutch West Indies in 1698, a mariner 'who stayed in the house of James Bell in Broad Street, Curacao', died on 29 January 1714. [ACA.APB.1.568]

MILNE, ROBERT, born on 22 April 1775, son of Reverend James Milne and his wife Jean, a merchant in St Domingo, died on 9 September 1814. [F.6.330]

MILNE, WILLIAM, born 1815, son of John Milne at the Mill of Boyndie near Banff, a Customs Collector, died at Old Harbour, Jamaica, on 7 May 1850. [AJ]

MITCHELL, JOHN, born 1780, son of Reverend Dr Mitchell in Kinellar, Aberdeenshire, Captain of the Britannia a West Indiaman, in Trinidad on 1 March 1811. [AJ]

MITCHELL, JOHN, a merchant in Glasgow, trading with Jamaica, Demerara, Trinidad, New York, Nova Scotia, and Quebec, in 1818. [NRS.CS96.3457]

MITCHELL, THOMAS, of Jamaica, graduated MD from Glasgow University in 1835. [RGG]

MITCHELL, WILLIAM, master of the Peggy from St Croix bound for North Faro but was shipwrecked at Torrisdale in Sutherland by 1781. [NRS.HCAS.AC7.58]

MOIR, GEORGE, only son of Reverend William Moir in Fyvie, Aberdeenshire, settled in Kingston, Jamaica, died in Surrey on 11 September 1807. [AJ]

MOIR, JOHN, son of Thomas Moir and his wife Christian Ross in Aberdeenshire, settled in Curacao, Dutch West Indies, in 1700. [ACA.APB]. [NRS.CS284.191]

MOIR, JOHN, formerly a writer [lawyer] in Alloa, Clackmananshire, later in Kingston, Jamaica, a petition in 1881

MOIR, WILLIAM, born on 5 October 1777, son of George Moir in Cruden, Peterhead, Aberdeenshire, was educated at King's College in Aberdeen, around 1792, a writer [lawyer] in Edinburgh and in Trinidad. [KCA]

MONRO, GEORGE, son of George Monro in Berbice deceased, a student at King's College, Aberdeen, around 1825. [KCA]

MONTGOMERIE, JAMES, Governor of Dominica in 1803. [NRS.GD143.45]

MONTGOMERY, JOHN, a merchant in Port Glasgow by 1795, formerly in Tortula around 1794, purchased a French prize the 200 ton brigantine La Fleur in 1794. [NRS.AC7.67]

MONTGOMERIE, ROBERT, from Irvine in Ayrshire, a merchant on St Croix, partner of Owen Eivers, a merchant on St Thomas, and St Croix, records from 1809 until 1829. [NRS.CS96.4488]

MONTIER, JAMES, master of the Pelican of Saltcoats from Saltcoats via Cork to Barbados and Antigua and return to Glasgow in 1734. [NRS.HCAS. AC7.40.166]

MOORE, ADRIANA, daughter of William Moore in St Eustatia, Dutch West Indies, married Robert Semple, from Demerara, in Glasgow on 3 September 1817. [BM.2.126]

MOOR, ANDREW, was aboard the Walter of Glasgow in September 1682 when it returned from the Caribbean. [NRS.E72.19.5]

MOORE, ELIZABETH, from St Eustatia, married James McInry from Demerara, in Broomloan, on 25 December 1797. [EEC.420]

MORGAN, GORDON, purchased land in St Kitts in 1765. [NRS.GD1.32.38.27]

MORGAN, Dr WILLIAM, former Rector of Kingston, Jamaica, late Professor of Philosophy at Marischal College in Aberdeen, testament, 12 February 1789 Comm. Aberdeen. [NRS]

MORRISON, CHRISTOPHER, a sailor from Greenock, died upon the Dolphin at Darien, Panama, in 1699, testament, 1707, Comm. Edinburgh. [NRS]

MORRISON, GEORGE, in St Lucy's, Barbados, in 1679. [TNA.CO1.44/47]

MORRISON, WILLIAM, a surgeon in Banff who emigrated to Jamaica in 1784. [PSAS.114.495]

MORRISON, WILLIAM, son of Theodore Morrison and his wife Catherine Maitland in Bognie, Fyvie, Aberdeenshire, was educated at King's College in Aberdeen, a barrister in Quebec, married Catherine de Bronyac, settled in Grenada, Chief Justice of the Bahamas, died in Nassau. [TOF.156] #

MORN, DAVID, from Glasgow, married Marjory Stevenson, youngest daughter of Robert Stevenson a farmer in Auchanachie, Banffshire, in the British Consulate in Mexico City, in 1859. [CM.21776]

MORRIS, ALEXANDER BRUCE, died in Berbice on 20 July 1808. [SM.70.796]

MORRISON, ALEXANDER, born 1826 in Turriff, Aberdeenshire, died of fever in Kingston, St Vincent, on 1 November 1863. [AJ]

MORRISON, JAMES, MD, born in Inverurie, served in the East India Company, then a farmer in Alford, settled in Grenada in 1858, died there on 2 January 1860. [AJ]

MORSON, WALTER SKERRET, M.D., from Montserrat, married Jane Jameson, daughter of Robert Jameson a Writer to the Signet, in Edinburgh, on 25 October 1822. [S.302.348]

MOWAT, CHARLES EGGLESTONE, son of James Mowat a merchant in Aberdeen, died in Tobago on 27 February 1836. [AJ]

MOWAT, JAMES, son of James Mowat a merchant in Aberdeen, died in Demerara on 21 January 1838. [AJ]

MUDIE, WILLIAM, from Glasgow, was drowned off Surinam on 18 October 1822. [DPCA]

MUIR, JAMES, of Todd, Muir, and Company, died in Vera Cruz, Mexico, on 6 September 1834. [SG.2.192]

MUIR, JAMES, an engineer in Demerara, son and heir of John Muir a millwright in Paisley, Renfrewshire, who died on 12th January 1844. [NRS.S/H]

MUIR, JOHN, son of John Muir in Greenhall, died in Demerara on 5 August 1808. [SM.71.78]

MUIR, Mrs, widow of John Muir in Demerara, married Daniel Mackay from St Croix in the Danish West Indies, in Morningside, Edinburgh, on 17 February 1825. [BM.17.638]

MUNRO, ALEXANDER, in Demerara, a Power of Attorney in favour of C. R. Manson, dated 15 September 1829. [NRS.RD403.639]

MUNRO, ARTHUR, only son of James Munro in Scotsburn, Ross-shire, died in Demerara on 16 November 1849. [IA]

MUNRO, DENNIS, in St Lucy's, Barbados, in 1679. [TNA.CO1.44/47]

MUNRO, GEORGE, a student at Marischal College in Aberdeen in 1822, son of the late George Munro in Berbice in 1822, [MCA]; from Berbice, died in Falmouth, England, on 22 June 1824. [DPCA.1149]

MUNRO, JAMES, in St Phillip's parish in Barbados in 1680. [TNA.CO1.44/47]

MUNRO, JOHN, in St Lucy's, Barbados, in 1679. [TNA.CO1.44/47]

MUNRO, M., was granted the Edinburgh Plantation in Berbice in 1792. [TNA]

MUNRO, Dr WILLIAM, from Easter Ross, a planter in Demerara in 1798. [RSSP.104]; a planter in Berbice by 1802. [RSSP.105]

MUNRO, MANSON, & Company. in Demerara, a deed in favour of J. Campbell & Company, dated 13 January 1830. [NRS.RD403.636]

MURRAY, GEORGE, son of James Murray in Jamaica, was educated at Marischal College in Aberdeen around 1844, later a newspaper editor. [MCA]

MURRAY, HENRY N., from Antigua, graduated MD from Edinburgh University in 1825. [EMG]

MURRAY, JAMES, MA, an alumni, minister of St George's, Bermuda, graduated DD at King's College, Aberdeen, on 28 September 1841. [KCA]

MURRAY, PATRICK, an officer of the 60th [Royal American] Regiment in Jamaica in 1776. [IRO][TNA.WO]

MURRAY, THOMAS, master of the Walmington at Jamaica in 1755. [NRS.HCAS.AC7.48.595]

MURRAY, WILLIAM, in Mexico, a Deed of Factory to Mrs Mary Murray dated 8 April 1861. [NRS.RD5.1128.382/74]

MURROE, JOHN, in St Joseph's, Barbados, in 1680. [TNA.CO1.44/47]

NANTON, JOHN, purchased land in Antigua in 1765. [NRS.GD1.32.38.27]

NEALE, Count, a letter regarding his property transferred from Surinam, dated 22 June 1798. [NRS.NRAS.1798]

NEILL, WILLIAM, son of William Neill, a carpenter in Demerara, died in January 1832. [NRS.P3.15.167/462]

NICHOLSON, ADAM, born 1819, from Antigua, graduated MD from Glasgow University in 1845, died on 6 June 1868. [RGG]

NICOL, FRANCIS, a student at Marischal College in Aberdeen around 1800, son of Kenneth Nicol in Tobago. [MCA]

NEWBURN, THOMAS, in Demerara, a letter from Thomas Cumming late from Demerara now in Elgin, Moray, dated 1799. [NRS.GD23.6.364]

NISBIT, JAMES, took the Association Oath in Antigua on 14 May 1696. [TNA]

NISBET, P., a planter in Aurora, Essequibo, deeds in 1802. [NRS.RD3.298.262; RD3.298.256]

NISBET, PETER, a merchant in Demerara, son of Peter Nisbet in Glasgow, died in Demerara, on 12 August 1802. [SM.64.859]

NIVEN, HUGH, formerly a merchant in Glasgow, died in Demerara in January 1803. [EEC.14299]

NOBLE, AGNES, in Jamaica, a sasine, 2 December 1815. [NRS.RS.Queensferry.1.85]

NOBLE, JOHN, owner of Plantation Mary Ville in Essequibo, a letter concerning his son's education at Inverness Academy, dated1813, [NRS.GD23.6.527]; he died before 5 October 1820. [NRS.GD23.6.613]

NOBLE, WALTER, master of the Mayflower of Glasgow from Port Glasgow on 3 March 1685 bound for the Caribbean. [NRS.E72.19.9]

NURSE, JOHN, son of John Bailey Nurse in Barbados deceased, a student at King's College, Aberdeen, in 1825. [KCA]

OATES, ROBERT, son of George Oates a planter in Jamaica, graduated MB from Marischal College in Aberdeen in 1853. [MCA]

OGILVIE, GEORGE, late of Jamaica, a trust disposition dated 4 July 1808. [NRS.CH2.1218.73]

OGILVIE, JOHN, born 1753, son of William Ogilvie and his wife Helen Baird in Banff, died in Antigua on 30 August 1770. [Banff gravestone]

OGILVIE, PATRICK, born 12 September 1774, son of John Ogilvie in Midmar, Aberdeenshire, was educated at King's College in Aberdeen from 1787 until 1791, a surgeon in St Domingo. [KCA]

OGILVIE, JAMES, born 1747, son of William Ogilvie and his wife Helen Baird in Banff, died in Jamaica on 6 June 1774. [Banff gravestone]

OGILVIE, JOHN, born 1753, son of William Ogilvie and his wife Helen Baird in Banff, died in Antigua on 30 August 1770. [Banff gravestone]

OGILVIE, PATRICK, born 12 September 1774, son of John Ogilvie in Midmar, Aberdeenshire, was educated at King's College in Aberdeen from 1787 until 1791, a surgeon in St Domingo. [KCA]

O'MEALLY, PATRICK, of Jamaica, graduated CM from Glasgow University in 1825. [RGG]

OLIPHANT, THOMAS, a sailor from Shetland, died aboard the Caledonia at Darien, Panama, in 1698, testament 1707, Comm. Edinburgh. [NRS]

ORR, Captain SAMUEL, son of James Orr a merchant in Leith, died in Kingston, Jamaica, on 9 July 1813. [SM.75.959]

OTTLEY, RICHARD, purchased land in Antigua in 1765. [NRS.GD1.32.38.27]

OUGHTERSON, ARTHUR, and Company in Greenock, trading with Demerara in 1817. [NRS.CS96.4618]

OWENS, THOMAS, master of the Sea Flower of Leith died in Jamaica, testament, 1740, Comm. Edinburgh. [NRS].

PARK, BREADIE, from Greenock in Renfrewshire, died in Kingston, Jamaica, in 1811. [EA.4977]

PARK, GEORGE, born on 3 November 1777 in Dunnottar, Kincardineshire, son of William Park and his wife Rebecca Middleton, died in Guadaloupe in 1807. [Fetteresso gravestone, Kincardineshire]

PARK, JAMES, a planter in Jamaica, son of Walter Park, a cooper in Greenock, in 1807. [NRS.S/H]

PARKER, CHARLES STEWART, born 1771, son of a Scottish merchant, in Norfolk, Virginia, an apprentice in Grenada from 1789, a partner in Sandbach, Tinne and Company in 1792, married Margaret Rainy or Creich, died in 1828. [RSSP.116]

PARKINSON, ANN, married Robert Gordon of Hope Estate in Demerara on 3 June 1804. [SM.66.806]

PATERSON, CHARLES, a student at Marischal College in Aberdeen around 1821, son of George Paterson MD in Grenada. [MCA]

PATERSON, JAMES, a student at Marischal College in Aberdeen around 1820, son of George Paterson MD in Grenada. [MCA]

PATTERSON, JOHN WINTER, born 1815, son of Robert Patterson in Demerara, was educated at Edinburgh Academy from 1824 to 1828. [EAR]

PATERSON and CAMPBELL, merchants in Glasgow, trading with Demerara from 1812 until 1816. [NRS.CS96.3460]

PATRICK, JAMES, master of the Sally trading between Dundee and Grenada in 1773, and in 1775. [NRS.E504.11.8]

PAULL, JOHN ALEXANDER, born 1842, son of George Paull of Newseat, died on Calder Estate, St Vincent, on 30 June 1868. [AJ]

PEDDIE, ANDREW, master of the <u>Elizabeth of Dundee</u>, from Dundee via Rotterdam bound for Madeira and Savanna la Mar in Jamaica on 23 December 1775. [NRS.E504.11.9]

PENISTON, JAMES, purchased land in St Eustatius in 1765. [NRS.GD1.32.38.27]

PETERKIN, J. D., a merchant in Glasgow, trading with Demerara from 1807 until 1810. [NRS.CS96.1494]

PIRIE, ANDREW, born 1797 in Aberdeen, died in St John's. Antigua on 22 June 1871. [AJ]

POLLARD, THOMAS F., of Demerara, graduated MD from Glasgow University in 1842. [RGG]

POLLOCK, WALTER, a student at Marischal College in Aberdeen about 1818, son of Walter Pollock in Jamaica. [MCA]

POLSON, HENRY, born 1830 son of John Polson in Old Aberdeen, died in Barbados on 28 January 1855. [AJ]

PORTER, Dr WILLIAM, agent at Lochbay for the British Fishery Society, moved to Jamaica but was captured by the French on the return journey, letters from 1802 until 1810. [NRS.GD9.166]

PORTER, WILLIAM, born 1816, son of Francis Porter in Auchintender, Forgue, died at Mount Pleasant, St Vincent on 22 February 1847. [AJ]

POTTS, THOMAS, born 1738, senior magistrate in Berbice for 45 years, died there in 1806. [SM.69.158]

POWRIE, WILLIAM, a receipt for £143 10 shillings received from Alexander Hay to finance the journey to Barbados, dated 4 February 1639. [NRS.GD504.9.97/6]; took the Association Oath in Nevis in 1696. [TNA]

PRINGLE, WILLIAM, a planter in Surinam in 1675, 1676, [SPAWI,1675/1; 1676/943]

PRINGLE, WILLIAM, a merchant in Surinam, trading with John Drummond of Quarrel, a Scottish merchant in Amsterdam, letters dated 1725. [NRS.GD24.1.464]

PRYDE, DAVID, born 1853, son of David Pryde in Tayport, Fife, died of yellow fever in Havanna, Cuba, on 8 May 1873. [PJ]

PYPER, JAMES, born 1840, son of John Pyper of 106 King Street, Aberdeen, died of yellow fever in Georgetown, Demerara, on 1 September 1864. [AJ]

QUARREL, WILLIAM DAWES, in Jamaica, versus Robert Dunmore and Company, merchants in Glasgow, 1780. [NRS.HCAS.AC7.57]

RAINY, GEORGE, born around 1785, from Creich in Sutherland, a merchant in Demerara from 1806, later a partner in Sandwich, Tinne, and Company, died in 1864. [RSSP.116]

RAE, JOHN, born 1814, died in Antigua in 1835. Kirkcudbright gravestone]

RAMAGE, ALEXANDER, master of the Concord of Leith arrived in Anstruther in Fife on 24 July 1766 from Boston, New England. [NRS.E504.3.4]

RAMSAY, GILBERT, Rector of Christchurch in Barbados, soujourneying in Bath, England, his testament dated 21 February 1727. [NRS.CH1.2.72/138-267]

RAMSAY, JAMES, of Demerara, died in St Kitts on 14 May 1779. [SM.41.455]

RAMSEY, JOHN, in St Phillip's parish in Barbados in 1680. [TNA.CO1.44/47]

REED, BAYNES, of Barbados, graduated MD from Edinburgh University in 1825. [EMG]

REID, GEORGE, a Lieutenant Colonel of Militia in Kingston, Jamaica, in 1776. [IRO][TNA.WO]

REID, GEORGE, son of James Reid of Ardoch, died in Bellfield Estate, Demerara, on 26 July 1819. [S.145.19]

REID, HUGH, on the Unity of Ayr which returned to Ayr on 2 September 1673 from Montserrat. [NRS.E72.3]

REID, ROBERT, probably from Aberdeenshire, an overseer in Carriacou in the Grenadines from 1773. [PSAS.114.489]

REID, THOMAS LIDDLE, a baker in San Fernando, Trinidad, versus Mrs Sarah Shepherd or Reid in Glasgow, a Decree of Divorce, dated July 1893. [NRS.CS46.1893.7.93]

RICHARD, MELVILL, Captain of the Jane of Glasgow, son of William Richard and his wife Catherine Bell, died at the Black River, Jamaica, on 26 July 1817. [St Andrews gravestone, Fife] 48

RICHARDSON, ROBERT, in Nassau, New Providence in the Bahamas, deceased by1819, father of James Richardson in Perth, a letter dated 19 June 1819. [NRS.B59.38.5.63]

RICKETTS, SAMUEL, a merchant in Surinam, father of Thomas Ricketts, a student in 1815, and Samuel, a student in 1816, both at the University of Glasgow. [MAGU]

RITCHIE, Reverend DAVID, born 1753 in Perth, emigrated to Dominica in 1801, later in St George, Grenada. [EMA.52] [GM.72.181]

ROBB, ALEXANDER, from Old Machar in Aberdeenshire, was educated at King's College in Aberdeen, a Doctor of Divinity, minister of the United Presbyterian Church in Jamaica. [KCA]

ROBB, INGLIS, was manager of Robb and Inglis merchants in Demerara, sederunt book, 1825 to 1826. [NRS.CS96.378]

ROBERTSON, ALEXANDER, from Old Meldrum, resided in Jamaica for 28 years, died there in 1837. [AJ]

ROBERTSON, ARCHIBALD, fifth son of Charles Robertson of Kindeace, died in Demerara in 1795. [SM.57.133]

ROBERTSON, GEORGE, born 1756, a merchant in Grenada by the late 1780s, a partner of Sandbach, Tinne and Company in Guyana in 1792, died in 1799. [RSSP.116]

ROBERTSON, HENRY, in Esquibo, a probative will in favour of his sisters, dated 23 May 1830. [NRS.RD417.651]

ROBERTSON, LEONARD, master of the Margaret of Dundee from Dundee in March 1700 bound for Darien in Panama. [NRS.GD406]

ROBERTSON, Reverend ROBERT, born 18 March 1682 in Edinburgh, Rector of St Paul's, Charles Town, Nevis fom 1707, died 6 April 1739. [St Paul's gravestone][SPAWI.1727.771xi][FPA.275]

ROBERTSON, WILLIAM, a planter on Lejuen Island in Essequibo, in 1812. [NRS.RD5.129.194]

ROBINSON, ANDREW HAY, son of Dr James Robinson in Demerara, died there in 1819. [S.139.19]

ROBINSON, Dr JAMES, died in Demerara on 4 December 1808. [SM.71.238]

ROLLOCK, ANDREW, in St Lucy's, Barbados, in 1679. [TNA.CO1.44/47]

ROLLOCK, THOMAS, with his wife and children, died in Guadaloupe in the French West Indies before 1656. [GAA.1306.214]

ROSE, ALEXANDER, a surgeon, son of John Rose the Customs Collector of Thurso in Caithness, died in Berbice on 23 August 1802. [EA.4056.02]

ROSE, ANDREW, seventh son of William Rose of Gask in Aberdeenshire, Secretary to the Council, did at Mount Rose in St Vincent on 19 February 1822. [AJ]

ROSE, HARRIET, daughter of James Rose the Deputy Clerk of Session, died in Demerara on 16 September 1822. [BM.12.803]

ROSE, HUGH, the Deputy Quartermaster General of Martinique on 12 March 1796. [NRS.GD18.2262]

ROSE, MARY, eldest daughter of James Rose the Deputy Clerk of Session, married Colin Campbell from Demerara, in Edinburgh on 10 July 1821. [EA.6032.183]

ROSE, ROBERT, son of John Rose of Ormly, died in Demerara on 11 January 1805. [SM.67.565]

ROSS, ANDREW, fourth son of Hugh Ross of Kerse, died in Berbice on 26 September 1820. [BM.8.482]

ROSS, DAVID, MD, father of a daughter born in Nickerie, Dutch Guiana on 16 April 1870. [S.835]

ROSS, GEORGE, a magistrate in Demerara in 1843, son of Charles Ross a merchant in Aberdeen. [NRS.S/H]

ROSS, GEORGE, a plantation manager in Jamaica, a letter dated 20 December 1792. [NRS.GD248.977.2]

ROSS, JOHN, from Nigg in Easter Ross, a planter in Nigg in Berbice in 1802. [RSSP.105]; died there on 16 July 1807. [SM.68.958][DPCA.270]

ROSS, ROBERT, from Surinam, married Margaret Elizabeth Mitchell, daughter of Alexander Mitchell of Gargrgo, at Troqueer Holm on 15 September 1813. [SM.75.799]

ROSS, R., from Tain in Ross-shire, died in Trinidad on 6 November 1851. [IA]

ROSS, Captain, master of the Hopewell from Honduras to Leith with merchandise in 1795. [NRS.AC7.67]

ROSS, Captain, a shipmaster from Aberdeen to Antigua on 3 March 1752. [AJ]

ROWAN, Captain, master of the Alexander and James from Greenock bound for St Kitts with a cago of balegoods and herring in 1758. [AJ]D

ROWLEY, O., and his wife in Grenada, discharged H. Rose on 16 January 1832. [NRS.RD458.349.6]

RUDDACH, THOMAS, in Jamaica, a letter dated 1777. [NLS.ms5030.8]

RUDDIMAN, WALTER, son of Thomas Ruddiman a printer in Edinburgh, a midshipman aboard HMS Venus died in the West Indies on 10 May 1813. [SM.75.478]

RUSSELL, DAVID, son of David Russell and his wife Mary Black, died in Jamaica on 24 April 1867. [St Andrews gravestone, Fife]

RUSSELL, WILLIAM G., a bookkeeper in Jamaica, a sasine dated 17 December 1883. [NRS.R.S.Kirkcaldy, Fife, 21.14]

'ROYS, PIETER', a Scottish merchant in Surinam around 1680. [Archieven.nl.239]

RUSSEL, ERROL, born 1773, son of Thomas Russel of Rathen and Anna Innes his wife, a Lieutenant of the Royal Navy, died in the West Indies in July 1795. [Banff gravestone]

RUSSELL, JAMES, purchased land in Dominica in 1765.
[NRS.GD1.32.38.27]

RUSSELL, RODDAM, born in 1781, son of Tho. mas Russel of Rathen in Aberdeenshire, and his wife Anna Innes, a midshipman, died on 31 October 1797 in St Domingo. [Banff gravestone]

RUSSELL, Major R., in Antigua on 3 October 1783, a sasine.
[NRS.RS.Elgin and Forres.71]

RUSSEL, THOMAS, born 1772, son of Thomas Russel of Rathen Aberdeenshire, and Anna Innes his wife, died in Martinique in July 1794. [Banff gravestone]

SCALES, ANDREW, the younger, a merchant in Leith, trading with Demerara in 1807 to 1818. [NRS.CS96.783]

SCOBIE, ANGUS, son of Kenneth Scobie of Achmore in Sutherland, died in Demerara on 11 December 1807. [SM.70398]

SCOTT, ANDREW, son of Andrew Scott of Knockbog Grange, attorney on Westerhall Estate, Grenada, died there on 17 September 1844. [AJ]

SCOTT, CARTERET, at Montego Bay, Jamaica, a letter re the situation in San Domingo, dated 25 June 1793. [NRS.GD113.5.41.12]

SCOTT, COLIN PATRICK, second son of Reverend John Scott in Muthill, Perthshire, died in Antigua in July 1794. [SM.56.588]

SCOTT, DAVID a merchant in Antigua, a deed in 1779.
[NRS.RD4.226.1004]

SCOTT, JOHN, in Demerara, son of John Scott a merchant in Kincardine on Forth, a deed dated 20 February 1802. [NRS.RD3.295.657]

SCOTT, JOHN, of Tobago, graduated MD at Glasgow University in 1840. [RGG]

SCOTT, PATRICK, was born in Teviotdale in 1703, mate aboard the Dove from St Kitts to London in 1728. [TNA.HCA.Rex versus Scott in 1731]

SCOTT, WILLIAM HENRY, a merchant in St Eustatia, son of Alexander Scott a merchant in Edinburgh, died in Antigua on 12 May 1789.
[GM.XII.601.212]

SCOTT, Mrs, wife of Reverend James Scott, from Peterhead, Aberdeenshire, died in Demerara on 12 January 1836. [AJ]

SCRIMGEOUR, HARRY, a planter in Hanover parish, Jamaica by 1783. [NRS.NRAS.87.97.89.13]

SELKRIG, ROBERT, from Demerara, died in Edinburgh on 5 March 1823. [SM.111.520]

SEMPLE, ROBERT, from Demerara, married Adriana Moore, daughter of William Moore in St Eustatia, in Glasgow on 30 September 1817. [BM.2.126]

SERVICE, Captain, master of the John and Anne of Irvine, when bound from Irvine to Barbados was captured by a French privateer and taken to Bayonne on 2 April 1748. [AJ]

SHAND, GEORGE, formerly in Demerara late in Aberdeen, his widow Mary Walker's testament, 28 September 1793, Comm. Aberdeen. [NRS]

SHAND, JOHN, a student at Marischal College in Aberdeen around 1817, son of John Shand in Jamaica. [MCA]

SHAND, JOHN, a merchant in the West Indies, died in 1825. [Fettercairn, Kincardineshire]

SHAND, JOHN, trustees in Jamaica, a probative assignment to J. Sandeman on 23 January 1832. [NRS,RD4.5318]; trustees in Jamaica granted R. B. Shand a probative assignment on 16 November 1832. [NRS.RD471.561]

SHANNON, LIVINGSTON, and Company in Newfoundland, trading with Jamaica, New Providence, New York, Canada, Demerara, and the United States, from 1816 until 1817. [NRS.CS96.905.1]

SHARP, CHARLES, purchased land in Antigua in 1765. [NRS.GD1.32.38.27]

SHARP, JOHN, master of the Leith Galley, from Leith to Jamaica on 9 February 1755. [AJ]

SHARP, EMILIA, in Jamaica, a tack [lease] dated 7 April 1831. [NRS.RD438.755]

SHAW, LACHLAN, born on 27 January 1729, son of Reverend Lachlan Shaw and his wife Ann Grant, settled in Jamaica, died in London. [F.6.390]

SHAW, JAMES, master of the brig Venus of Port Glasgow a witness in Antigua in June 1779. [NRS.RD3.308.5]

SHAW, JOHN, a ship's carpenter aboard the Hunter of Port Glasgow, died in Grenada on 21 August 1794. Testament, 1795, Comm. Edinburgh. [NRS]

SHEDDEN, WILLIAM, in Bermuda and New York, letters, 1780-1784. [NRS.GD1.67.1]

SHERRIFS, DAVID, in St David's Park, Jamaica, an Assemblyman and Lieutenant Colonel of the Jamaica Militia, second son of David Sherrifs in Aberdeen, died in Kingston, Jamaica, on 4 September 1805. [AJ]

SHIRREFF, ROBERT, the younger, in St Croix, in the Danish West Indies, in 1849. [NRS.CS313.13]

SHIELDS, Reverend ALEXANDER, died 1700 in Jamaica, an elegy and epitaph. [NRS.CH1.5.1.81]

SIM, ANDREW, born in Ellon, Aberdeenshire, died on Plantation Garden of Eden in Demerara, on 7 August 1821. [BM.10.609]

SIM, JOHN, born 1744, late of Jamaica, died on 29 November 1807. [Banff gravestone]

SIMS, WILLIAM, in San Juan, Cuba, died on 21 March 1860, testament Edinburgh, 1862. [NRS].

SIMPSON, ANN, daughter of the deceased James Simpson, married James McIntosh, then a tutor later a minister in Dominica, on 13 March 1769, parents of David McIntosh born 16 April 1769, versus the said James McIntosh in a Process of Divorce in 1773. [NRS.CC8.6.531]

SIMPSON, JAMES, from Tobago, was admitted as a burgess of Banff in 1773. [BBR]

SIMPSON, JOHN, in Demerara, a deed dated 1814. [NRS.GD5,182,697]

SIMPSON, ROWLAND, a planter in Surinam around 1680. [SPAWI.291/402]

SINCLAIR, ARCHIBALD, in Jamaica, a letter to Sir Robert Gordon dated 25 June 1760. [EUL. Laing Charters ii.498]

SINCLAIR, JAMES, an army officer in St Pierre, Martinique, letters to Alexander Bower of Kincaldrum in Angus, in 1796. [NRS.GD503.151]

SIVEWRIGHT, JOHN HENRY, born 1847, son of C. K. Sivewright in Burntisland in Fife, died in Orange Valley, Falmouth, Jamaica, on 23 August 1865. [FJ]

SKAKLE, JOHN, born 1844, son of John Skakle a jeweller on St Nicholas Street, Aberdeen, died of yellow fever in Georgetown, Demerara, on 22 July 1865. He was Chief Officer aboard the <u>Kiltearn of Liverpool.</u> [AJ]

SKENE, Captain ANDREW, of the Royal Scots Regiment, died in Jamaica on 30 March 1742. [FSS.58]

SKENE, PHILIP WHARTON, was born on 5 February 1725, enlisted in the Royal Scots and served in Jamaica around 1742. [FSS.58]

SKENE, WILLIAM, son of William Skene [died 1856] a carpenter, and his wife Isabella MacLoorie [1786-1834], in Taymouth, Perthshire, died in Honduras in 1848. [Kenmore gravestone, Perthshire]

SKINNER, GEORGE URE, born 1805, second son of the Very Reverend John Skinner, Dean of Dunkeld and Dunblane, settled in Guatemala, died in Aspinwall, Panama, on 9 February 1862. [AJ][S.7342]

SMITH, JAMES BLACK, born 1857 son of John Smith and his wife Isabella Walker, died in Antigua on 23 August 1917. [St Andrews Cathedral gravestone, Fife]

SMITH, JOHN PRINCE, a barrister at law, second fiscal, King's Advocate in the United Colony of Demerara and Essequibo, died in Demerara in 1822. [BM.12.522]

SMITH, JOHN, a surgeon, died in Berbice on 14 December 1822. [DPCA.1130]

SMITH, JOHN, formerly in Antigua, lately in Cherryvale near Aberdeen, testament, 9 July 1795, Comm. Aberdeen. [NRS]

SMITH, JOHN, a missionary, who was imprisoned in the Colonial Gaol in Demerara, died there on 6 February 1829. [DPCA.1130]

SMITH, JAMES, born 1698, a mariner, husband of Isobel Lawson, died in Antigua in 1745. [Arbroath Abbey gravestone]

SMITH, JOHN, master of the Jean of Ely in Fife, from Anstruther in Fife, to St Kitts in January 1771. [NRS.E504.3.4]

SMITH, JOHN, formerly in Antigua, lately in Cherryvale near Aberdeen, testament, 9 July 1795, Comm. Aberdeen. [NRS]

SMITH, JOHN, born 1840, son of William D. Smith and his wife Janet Morrison, died in Nickerie, Surinam, on 16 May 1872. [Burntisland gravestone, Fife]

SMITH, NEIL, born 1823, son of A. Philips of Union Row, Aberdeen, died in Demerara of fever on 13 December 1842. [AJ]

SMITH, WILLIAM, in Martinique, letter dated 1 August 1795. [NRS.GD1.1.652]

SMITH, ..., master of the brigantine Page of Glasgow which was destroyed by a hurricane in Jamaica on 11 September 1751. [A

SPEARS, JOHN, son of Henry Spears in Auchtertool in Fife, died at Green River in Jamaica on 30 September 1837. [FH]

SPROAT, SAMUEL, in Demerara before 1813. [NRS.S/H]

SPURRILL, JOHN, master of the Mayflower of London, from Scotland with 108 passengers bound for Barbados, arrived there on 5 December 1698. [TNA.CO3.13]

STAFFORD, Dr JACKSON, purchased land in St Kitts in 1765. [NRS.GD1.32.38.27]

STALKER, DUNCAN, from Tobago, lately the Killean parish in Argyll, 18 September 1798. [NRS.CC2.8.102/7; CC2.9.5.14]

STARK, ALEXANDER, master of the Hopefull Binning of Bo'ness from Leith to Darien in Panama on 12 May 1699, arrived there in August 1699. [NRS.GD406.1]

STEDMAN, Captain JOHN GABRIEL, an officer of the Scots Brigade in the Netherlands, later a soldier in British Guiana around 1800. [NRS.GD99.299.9/2]

STEIL, Captain, master of the Mayflower of Irvin99e, when bound from Irvine to Barbados was captured by a French privateer and taken to Bayonne on 2 April 1748. [AJ]

STEELE, WILLIAM, a planter in Demerara, a will subscribed in 1782. [NRS.GD1.47.1]

STEWART, DANIEL, a surgeon in Dominica, and Jean Murray, daughter of William Murray, a merchant in Edinburgh, a post-nuptial marriage contract dated 24 October 1777. [NRS.CS238.F.3/4]

STEWART, JAMES, from Grenada, died in Demerara on 1 February 1791. [SM.53.203]

STENNETT, GEORGE RADCLIFFE, of Jamaica, a student at King's College, Aberdeen, around 1819; graduated MD from Edinburgh University in 1826. [KCA][EMG]

STEVENSON, JAMES, from Beith, Ayrshire, later in Tobago, versus Campbell and McLean, merchants and clothiers in Glasgow in March 1836. [NRS.CS46.1836.3/79]

STEVENSON, JOHN, born in Melrose, Roxburghshire, the proprietor of the 'Guiana Chronicle of Georgetown, Demerara' was drowned in the River Orinocco on 25 August 1823. [BM.15.492]

STEWART, ALEXANDER, son of Alexander Stuart of Edinglassie, Lieutenant Colonel of the 3rd West India Regiment, died of yellow fever on 21 January 1800 in Barbados. [AJ]

STEWART, CLEMENTINA, daughter of Sir John Stewart of Grantully in Perthshire, and widow of George Seton in St Vincent, letters from 1799 until 1823. [NRS.GD24.1.402/9]

STEWARD, DANIEL, was buried in St Philip's, Barbados, on 18 September 1678. [TNA.CO1.44/47]

STEWART, DANIEL, a surgeon in Dominica, and Jean Murray, daughter of William Murray, a merchant in Edinburgh, a post-nuptial marriage contract dated 24 October 1777. [NRS.CS238.F.3/4]

STIRLING, ARCHIBALD, in Jamaica, a letter to his father dated 5 November 1789. [SRA.T-SK.11.3.127.1]

STIRLING, JAMES, settled in Jamaica in 1753 as a merchant and planter on Hampden in Trelawney parish, until 1761 when he returned to Scotland. [SRA.T-SK11.2]

STIRLING, JOHN, a merchant in Barbados, a letter to William Gordon and Company in Glasgow concerning Captain James Maxwell master of the Neptune of Glasgow in January 1731. [NRS.CS228.A.3.19/28]

STIRLING, ROBERT, emigrated to Jamaica in 1742, a planter in Frontier in St Mary's parish in 1748. [SRA.T-SK11.2]

STORIE, FRANCIS, a sailor from Linlithgow, West Lothian, died aboard the St Andrew in the West Indies in 1699, testament, 1707, Comm. Edinburgh. [NRS]

STORY, GEORGE, master of the John from Aberdeen to Grenada, St Kitts and Tortula on 20 December 1788. [AJ]

STRACHAN, ROBERT, born 1777, a shipwright who died in St Vincent in 1805. [Howff graveyard, Dundee]

STUART, JAMES GILLESPIE, second son of John Stuart the minister at Blair Atholl in Perthshire, died at Green Park in Jamaica on 23 August 1851, after 20 years residence in Jamaica. [IA][Falmouth Public Journal]

STUART, JOHN, in St Phillip's parish in Barbados in 1680. [TNA.CO1.44/47]

STUART, PATRICK, Lieutenant Colonel of the 3rd West Indies Regiment, son of Alexander Stuart of Edinglassie, died in Barbados on 21 January 1800. [AJ]

SUTHELAND, PETER, born in Ardersier, a carpenter, died inTrinidad on 7 December 1854. [IA]

TAIT, WILLIAM, ship's carpenter aboard the Molly of Glasgow bound for St Kitts in 1761. [NRS.AC7.50]

TAYLOR, JAMES, a sailor from Greenock, died on the Hope at Darien, Panama, in 1699, testament, 1707, Comm. Edinburgh. [NRS]

TEMPLE, MARGARET, widow of David Brown a shipbuilder in Leith, later in Martinique on 10 July 1799. [NRS.CS97.105.14]

TENNANT, JOHN, a merchant in St Kitts in 1765. [NRS.HCAS.7.51]

SUTHERLAND, ALEXANDER, born 1797 in Dornoch, Sutherland, died in Demerara in January 1830. [AC.20.3.1830]

SUTHERLAND of Fearquhar family, papers re Grenada, [NRS.GD347.111-118]

SWORD, THOMAS, in Antigua, a deed of commission with George and Henry Cairns dated on 14 August 1863. [NRS.RD118.735]

TAVERNER, HENRY, master of the 120 ton Martha of London arrived in Dunbarton on 29 January 1640 from the West Indies. [TNA.HCA.13/56.426]

TAYLOR, GEORGE, born 1831 in Inverurie, died in New Amsterdam, Berbice, Demerara, on 28 September 1860. [AJ]

TAYLOR, JOHN, in Jamaica, a bond in favour of Miss Meliss, dated 14 February 1830. [NRS.RD420.281]

TEASDALE, WILLIAM, a student at Marischal College in Aberdeen in 1820, son of William Teasdale a merchant in Jamaica. [MCA]

THAIN, JAMES WILSON, born 1824, late of Drumblair Cottage, died of fever at Snell Hall in Grenada on 28 December 1853. [AJ]

THIERENS MATTHIAS, from Essequibo, graduated MD from Glasgow University in 1816. [RGG]

THOMAS and STIRLING, merchants in Barbados, a letter to William Gordon and Company, merchants in Glasgow, regarding the slave trade and supplying lists of slaves sold and the names of their purchasers, dated July 1731. [NRS.CS228.A.3.19/33, 40, 41]

THOMSON, ANDREW, chief engineer with the West India Company. died on Buck Island in the West Indies on 29 October 1867. [DP]

THOMSON, ARCHIBALD, was proposed for the Council of Nevis in 1765. [SPAWI]

THOMSON, CHARLES, master of the Leith Galley arrived in Kingston, Jamaica, on 20 July 1751 from Leith, damaged there by a hurricane, returned to Leith in April 1752. [AJ]

THOMPSON, DAVID, a merchant tailor in Edinburgh, trading with Demerara from 1820 until 1822. [NRS.CS96.3592]

THOMSON, FRANCIS, born 27 April 1770, son of Reverend James Thomson and his wife Helen Anderson in Aberlour, Banffshire, a planter in St Vincent. [F.6.335]

THOMSON, GEORGE, born in Ellon, Aberdeenshire, in 1824, settled in Tobago in 1844, died there of fever on 24 November 1846. [AJ]

THOMSON, JOHN, born in Aberdeen in 1821, Captain of the barque <u>Ellon of London</u>, died at Port Morant in Jamaica on 8 February 1852. [AJ]

THOMSON, ROBERT, a surgeon, second son of Thomas Thomson the town clerk of Musselburgh in Midlothian, died in Demerara in February 1821. [BM.9.245]

THOMSON, THOMAS, son of Alexander Thomson a tobacconist in Edinburgh, an overseer on Plantation Plaisance on the east coast of Demerara, died on 2 May 1824. [DPCA.1146]

THOMSON, THOMAS, MD, born in Hamilton, Lanarkshire, in 1803, was drowned in the Pomeroon River, Guiana, on 3 June 1827. [S.789.488]

THOMSON, WILLIAM, son of baillie William Thomson in Aberdeen, settled in Jamaica, died in Philadelphia, Pennsylvania, on 3 July 1801. [AJ]

THORNTON, ELIZA, daughter of …Thornton in Cummingsburg, Guyana, married Captain MacDuff Hart Boog, in Demerara on 10 January 1820. [BM.7.231]

TOWER, ANNE, daughter of George Tower in Aberdeen, died on St Croix in the Danish West Indies on 8 January 1843. [AJ]

THOMPSON, DAVID, a merchant tailor in Edinburgh, trading with Demerara from 1820 until 1822. [NRS.CS96.3592]

THOMSON, WILLIAM, settled in Jamaica, son of baillie William Thomson in Aberdeen, died in Philadelphia, Pennsylvania, on 3 July 1801. [AJ]

TRIGGE, Lieutenant General, in Martinique, letters, 1790s. [NRS.GD46.17.21]

TROTTER, JOHN, a merchant in Kingston, Jamaica, in 1755. [NRS.HCAS.AC7.47.598]

TULLOCH, HENRY, a merchant in Demerara in 1806. [NRS.AC.77]

TURNBULL, Mrs, from Fochabers in Aberdeenshire, died in Demerara on 1 February 1801. [GC.1519]

TURNER, Sir H., in Bermuda, a letter re Lieutenant Hope of the 96th Regiment, dated 30 August 1826. [NRS.GD45.3.581]

TURNER, JOHN, son of John Turner of Turnerhall and his wife Elizabeth Urquhart, died in Grenada on 2 June 1792. [AJ]

TURNER, WILTON, born 1811, son of Dutton Turner in Jamaica, educated at Edinburgh Academy from 1824 to 1828. [EAR]

TYNDALL, SAMUEL, of Berbice, graduated MD From Edinburgh University in 1819. [EUL]

URQUHART, DUNCAN, a Captain of the 50th [Queen's Own] Regiment, stationed in Jamaica around 1776. [TNA.WO][IRO]

URQUHART, JOHN, born 1750, son of Captain John Urquhart of Craigston, and his wife Jean Urquhart of Meldrum, in Aberdeenshire, a planter on Carriacou in the Grenadines from 1772 until 1785. [PSAS.114.489-495]

URQUHART, ROBERT, born 1806, settled in Kingston, Jamaica, in 1827, eldest son of Alexander Urquhart a builder in Elgin, Moray, died in Jamaica on 26 October 1851. [IA]

URQUHART, WILLIAM, of Meldrum in Aberdeenshire, a planter in Carriacou in the Grenadines from 1775. [PSAS.114.482]

URQUHART, WILLIAM, born 1758, son of James Urquhart in Aberdeenshire, a surveyor in Carriacou in the Grenadines from 1771 until his death in 1790. [PSAS.114.519]

VAN WELL, MARTIN CHARLES, only son of August Van Well in Guiana, matriculated at Glasgow University in 1838, graduated MD in 1842. [RGG]

WADDELL, JAMES, born 1816, son of James Waddell a merchant in Jamaica, educated at Edinburgh Academy from 1824 to 1828. [EAR]

WALKER, JAMES FIFE, born 3 February 1814, son of Reverend Alexander Walker and his wife in Urquhart, Moray, a planter in Berbice, died on 6 August 1842. [F.6.411]

WALKER, JOHN, born 1822, son of Andrew Walker a farmer at Keithhll after only two weeks on the island', died in St Lucia on 8 December 1845, he was a clerk of Messrs McHugh and Company of St Lucia. [AJ] '

WALKER, W.P., a surgeon, son of David Walker a farmer at Upper Park, died in Grenada on 27 October 1838. [AJ]

WALKINSHAW, ROBERT, in Rancho del Oro in Mexico, brother and heir of Captain William Walkinshaw of the East India Service, 30 August 1827. [NRS.S/H]; also, heir to his cousin Euphemia Moffat in Kinghorn, Fife, 16 November 1846. [NRS.S/H]

WALKINGSHAW, WILLIAM, master of the Montrose from Jamaica with a cargo of sugar with a cargo of sugar to Greenock in November 1757, [AJ]; master of the Mary of Glasgow from Greenock bound for Jamaica on 29 November 1773, [NRS.CE60.1.7]; testament, 1784, Comm. Glasgow. [NRS]

WALLACE, or RIGSBY, AGNES, in Nottingham, England, sister and heir of William Wallace in Jamaica, 16 February 1788. [NRS.S/H]

WALLACE, Dr WILLIAM, of the Three Friends [Plantation?], died in Demerara on 2 November 1823. [BM.15.249]

WALLDEN, CHARLES, from Antigua, married Elizabeth Deys, in Edinburgh on 11 April 17--. [EMR]

WALLEN, JOHN, son of Matthew Wallen in Jamaica, a student at Marischal College in Aberdeen from 1773 until 1777. [MCA]

WALLIS, ELIZABETH, wife of Archibald Wallis, was buried in St Philip's, Barbados, on 30 July 1679. [TNA.CO1.44/47]

WAND, or BECK, JANET, widow of John N. Beck a planter in Antigua, grand-daughter and heir of William Wand the portioner of Pitgober, 26 March 1794. [NRS.S/H]

WARDEN, WILLIAM, a mariner aboard the Jean of Gourock to Jamaica before 1730. [NRS.9.1104]

WARDEN, Captain, master of the Industry from Greenock with a cargo of herring bound for Barbados on 1 December 1753. [AJ]

WATSON, JAMES, died on St Martins [St Maartens in the Dutch West Indies?] on 14 June 1804. [SM.66.644]

WATSON, ALEXANDER, son of Alexander Watson a book-seller in Aberdeen, died in Barbados on 10 December 1842. [AJ]

WATSON, ANDREW, a merchant in Greenock trading with Tortula in 1784. [NRS.AC7.61]

WATSON, JAMES, a merchant in Greenock, master of the Dove trading with Madeira, Barbados, Antigua and Virginia from 1741 until 1749. [NRS.CS96.1920]

WATSON, JAMES, died on St Martins [St Maartens in the Dutch West Indies?] on 14 June 1804. [SM.66.644]

WATSON, JAMES, from Aberdour, Aberdeenshire, was educated at King's College in Aberdeen around 1843, later minister of the United Presbyterian Church in Kingston, Jamaica. [KCA]

WATSON, JOHN, the younger, formerly a planter in Maryland and Virginia, a merchant in Edinburgh, trading with Martinique, Pennsylvania, Barbados and Jamaica, between 1696 and 1713. [NRS.CS96]

WATSON, ROBERT, master of the Grand Turk of Greenock from Greenock via the Canaries and Madeira to Barbados in November 1750. [NRS.E504.15.4]

WATSON, THOMAS, master of the Welcome of Greenock trading with Antigua in December 1742. [NRS.E504.151]

WATT, ALEXANDER, in St Phillip's parish in Barbados in 1680. [TNA.CO1.44/47]

WATT, DAVID, in St Phillip's parish in Barbados in 1680. [TNA.CO1.44/47]

WATT, JAMES, from Cairnie in Aberdeenshire, died on Montreuil Estate, Grenada, on 29 August 1863.

WATT, PETER, died 12 September 1865, his wife Agnes Glennie, from Inverurie, Aberdeenshire, died on George's Plain Estate, Savanna-la-Mar, Jamaica, on 8 September 1865. [AJ]

WAUCHOPE, PATRICK, a of the 50th [Queen's Own] Regiment, stationed in Jamaica around 1776. [TNA.WO][IRO]

WEIR, DANIEL, a merchant, son of Thomas Weir of Kerse, died in Demerara in 1793. [SM.55.153]

WEIR, WILLIAM, a merchant from Aberdeenshire, who settled in St James, Jamaica, and died by 1753. [ACA.APB]

WELSH, JOHN, a merchant in Jamaica in 1769. [NRS.HCAS.AC7.53]

WEST, JANET ANNE, second daughter of James E. West in Kingston, Jamaica, and grand-daughter of Mrs Hugh Kennedy of Battersea, Manchester, Jamaica, married Thomas Shepherd Hood from Cupar in Fife, in San Francisco on 29 October 1881. [FJ]

WHITE, JAMES, son of Robert White in Cupar, Fife, died in Demerara on 19 January 1856. [RH]

WHITE, MICHAEL, purchased land in Montserrat in 1765. [NRS.GD1.32.38.27]

WHITE, PATRICK, a merchant from Fraserburgh in Aberdeenshire, who emigrated before 1749, and died in the Leeward Islands in 1754. [ACA.ACA]

WHYTE, ARCHIBALD, master of the Peggy of Greenock bound via Guernsey to Antigua, was accused of 'wilfully casting the sloop away' in December 1782. [NRS.HCAS.AC9.3184]

WIGHTMAN, CHARLES, and ARCHIBALD SMITH, merchants in Tobago in 1780. [NRS.HCAS.AC7.57]

WIGHTMAN, CHARLES, in Tobago, a probative will, dated 18 July 1829. [NRS.RD429.629]

WILKIE, DAVID, was buried in St Philip's, Barbados, on 14 July 1678. [TNA.CO1.44-47]

WILLIAMS, ROBERT, master of the Barbados Merchant from Barbados, landed at Leith on 7 July 1665. [Acts PCCol.]

WILLIAMSON, ALEXANDER, a surgeon from Edinburgh, died in Montserrat on 29 August 1829. [BM.27.134]

WILLIAMSON, ALEXANDER, formerly in Jamaica, lately in Haugh of Edinglassie, Aberdeenshire, testament, 23 December 1796, Comm. Aberdeen. [NRS]

WILLIAMSON, MARGARET, born 1831, wife of Daniel Stewart, died in Acapulco, Mexico, on 3 September 1853. [Kirkcaldy gravestone, Fife]

WILSON, ADAM, son of John Wilson of Mountgrew, in Banffshire, died at Bossue, Manchester, Jamaica, on 10 November 1850. [AJ]

WILSON, JEANNIE, born 1846, daughter of Alexander Milne at the Mains of Esslemont, Aberdeenshire, died at St Joseph's, Trinidad on 16 December 1874. [AJ]

WILSON, JAMES, son of George Wilson and his wife Margaret Phillip in Banff, died in Port au Prince, Haiti, on 20 June 1794. [Banff gravestone]

WILSON, JOHN, MD, on St Martins [St Maartens in the Dutch West Indies?] married Catherine Thomson, daughter of John Thomson in Jamaica, in Glasgow on 7 November 1798. [GC.1122]

WILSON, JOHN, from Scotland, a planter in Berbice by 1802. [RSSP.105]

WILSON, JOHN, son of John Wilson of Mountgrew, in Banffshire, died at Draxhall, St Ann's Bay, Jamaica, on 5 December 1850. [AJ]

WILSON, ROBERT, in Jamaica granted his mother powers of attorney on 10 May 1832. [NRS.RD469.110]

WILSON, ROBERT SMITH, second son of James Wilson in Earlston, Berwickshire, died in Havanna, Cuba, in April 1873. [S.9315]

WILSON, Reverend STEPHEN HISLOP, MA, born 1854, youngest son of Robert Wilson in Duns, Berwickshire, died at Montego Bay, Jamaica, on 31 December 1898. [S.17342]

WILSON, WILLIAM, in Tobago, a deed dated 18 October 1830. [NRS.RD434.130]

WILSON, WILLIAM, son of William Wilson a writer [lawyer] in Edinburgh, died in Surinam on 6 August 1812. [SM.74.886]

WISHART, DANIEL, from Aberdeen, chief mate of the Barque <u>John King of Glasgow</u> died in Jamaica on 26 September 1857. [AJ]

WOOD, DAVID, master of the William and Elizabeth of Leith, witnessed a deed in Antigua in 1773. [NRS.RD3.232.432]

WOOD, JAMES GARDINER, of the Bote Mining Company in Zacatacas, Mexico, testament 1899, Edinburgh. [NRS.SC70.1.383.205]

WRIGHT, BUCHAN WANAN, son of Robert Wright MD in Jamaica, a student at King's College, Aberdeen, from 1825 to 1826, later a surgeon in the Honourable East India Company Service, graduated MD at Edinburgh University in 1837. [KCA]

WRIGHT, JOHN, a sailor from Keith in Banffshire, died on the St Andrew at Darien in Panama in 1698, testament 1707, Comm. Edinburgh. [NRS]

WRIGHT, JOHN, a merchant in Jamaica, was admitted as burgess of Ayr in 1751. [ABR]

WRIGHT, ROBERT, master of the Lord Frederick from Greenock to Tortula one of the Virgin Islands in April 1779. [NRS.E504.31]

WRIGHT, WILLIAM, a merchant in Stirling trading with Grenada in 1779. [NRS.CS16.1.175]

WYLLIE, ALEXANDER, son of Alexander Wyllie a weaver in Grahamshall, Orkney, a sailor aboard the Endeavour bound for Darien, Panama, in 1698, testament, 1707, Comm. Edinburgh. [NRS]

WYLLIE, HUGH, a merchant in Glasgow, trading with Barbados in 1765. [NRS.CS16.1.122]

WYLIE, JOHN, of Wylie, Cooke and Company, San Luis Potosi, Mexico, from 1830 to 1840. [GUL]

WYLLIE, Captain, master of the Grand Turk of Greenock from Greenock to Barbados in January 1750. [AJ]

YEAMAN, JOHN, purchased land in Antigua in 1765. [NRS.GD1.32.38.27]

YELTON, THOMAS, master of the Thomas and Betsey of Leith bound from Leith to Jamaica by July 1783. [NRS.HCAS.AC7.59]

YOUNG, ALEXANDER, a merchant in Aberdeen trading with the West Indies in 1769. [AJ]

YOUNG, DONALD, late of St Vincent, died at 63 St Vincent Crescent, Glasgow, on 6 November 1854. [IA]

YOUNG, FRANCIS, from Honduras, graduated MD from Edinburgh University in 1820. [EUL]

YOUNG, JAMES, born 1800 in Dundee, was educated at St Andrews University, a minister in British Guiana from 1841 until 1844, died in Broughty Ferry on 3 November 1882. [F.7.676]

YOUNG, JOHN, the younger, in Honduras, son of John Young a baker in Burntisland, Fife, and his wife Christian Wild, a deed dated 1804. [NRS.RD5.121.282]

YUILL, THOMAS, a merchant trading between Port Glasgow and Antigua in 1746. [NRS.E504.15.2]

www.ingramcontent.com/pod-product-compliance
Lightning Source LLC
Chambersburg PA
CBHW071459160426
43195CB00013B/2157